ALL IS CALM, ALL IS BRIGHT

True Stories of Christmas

Cheryl Kirking

Revell

a division of Baker Publishing Group
Grand Rapids, Michigan

© 2001, 2008 by Cheryl Kirking

Published by Revell
a division of Baker Publishing Group
P.O. Box 6287, Grand Rapids, MI 49516-6287
www.revellbooks.com

Printed in the United States of America

Library of Congress Cataloging-in-Publication Data
All is calm, all is bright : true stories of Christmas / [compiled by] Cheryl Kirking.
    p.   cm.
   ISBN 978-0-8007-3200-4
   1. Christmas—Anecdotes. I. Kirking, Cheryl, 1959–
BV45.A525   2001
242'.335—dc21   2001019534

Unless otherwise indicated Scripture quotations are from the HOLY BIBLE, NEW INTERNATIONAL VERSION®. NIV®. Copyright © 1973, 1978, 1984 by International Bible Society. Used by permission of Zondervan. All rights reserved.

Scripture marked KJV is taken from the King James Version of the Bible.

Scripture marked RSV is taken from the Revised Standard Version of the Bible, copyright 1952 [2nd edition, 1971] by the Division of Christian Education of the National Council of the Churches of Christ in the United States of America. Used by permission. All rights reserved.

ALL IS CALM,
ALL IS BRIGHT

To my parents,
Jean and LeVerne Kirking

CONTENTS

Preface   11
Acknowledgments   13

'ROUND YON VIRGIN MOTHER AND CHILD:
THE LIVING NATIVITY

Choirs Still Singing, Glories Still Streaming
    Bill Egan   17
The Mysterious Moving Nativity
    Cheryl Kirking   21
What Does Joe Do?
    Louisa Godissart McQuillen   23
Manger Babies   Linda LaMar Jewell   27
The Good Shepherd   Brenda Nixon   30
Where's the Baby Jesus?   Jeannie S. Williams   33

SLEEP IN HEAVENLY PEACE: TRANQUILITY RESTORED

The Bracelet Promise *Carmen Leal*   41

Full Circle *Raymond Flagg Jr.*   47

Goodwill on Earth *JudyAnn Squier*   50

Mystery Guest *James A. McClung*   53

Season of Love *Irene Bastian*   56

Christmas of My Dreams *Cheryl Kirking*   60

Chocolate-Covered Love *B. J. Taylor*   64

Tea Leaf Christmas *Mary Linn McClure*   67

GLORIES STREAM FROM HEAVEN AFAR: HE'S NEARER THAN YOU THINK

Is the Light in Your Eyes? *Cheryl Kirking*   73

All That Glitters Isn't Joy
   Lynn D. Morrissey   75

The Reminder *Marjorie K. Evans*   78

Flame of Love *Charlotte Adelsperger*   80

Let Every Heart Prepare Him Room
   Jessie Schut   83

Wish List *Cheryl Herndon*   86

A Christmas Miracle
   Kathleen Boratko Ruckman   89

The Year I Almost Missed Christmas
   Roberta L. Messner   94

CONTENTS

HEAV'NLY HOSTS SING ALLELUIA: ANGELS AMONG US

Little Red Wagon *Patricia Lorenz* 103
The Gift Twice Given *Patricia A. Perry* 108
Angels of Forgiveness *Susan M. Warren* 111
An Unlikely Angel *David Michael Smith* 115
And a Little Child Shall Lead Them
  Beverly M. Bartlett 120
The Snow Bunny
  Kathleen Boratko Ruckman 123
A Davy Crockett Hat for David
  Marjorie K. Evans 126
Real Class *Cheryl Kirking* 131

SON OF GOD, LOVE'S PURE LIGHT: PASSING IT ON

Christmas Mother *John W. Doll* 135
Christmas vs. a Cold Heart *Liz Hoyt* 142
When Receiving Is the Gift *Cheryl Kirking* 146
A Holiday Tradition *Pat A. Carman* 149
Oranges in Our Socks *Karin McClain* 152
Home for the Holidays *Margolyn Woods* 155
Spreading Christmas Cheer *John W. Doll* 158

With the Dawn of Redeeming Grace: Righteousness Revealed

Christmas Is . . . *Cheryl Kirking*   167

Evergreen *Jan Leong*   169

Seek and Ye Shall Find *Dianna Hutts Aston*   171

Thirsty *Joann Olson*   173

Christmas Stolen *Karen Igla*   175

The Christmas Robe *Valerie D. Howe*   179

Sweet Sounds of Gratitude *Sandra J. Bunch*   183

The Mutt and the Golden Retriever
   Cynthia Schaible Boyll   187

Saved *Cheryl Kirking*   190

Contributors   197

PREFACE

THIS HOLIDAY SEASON, untold millions across the globe will sing, in their own languages, "Silent night, holy night! All is calm, all is bright. . . ." Why has this song woven its way into hearts throughout the world? Because the words, set to a simple, lovely melody, remind us that we can find the peace we crave at Christmas and all the year through.

Although the origin of the song "Silent Night" has been dramatized by storytellers over the years, the unembellished story of its humble beginnings is beautiful in its simplicity. It is my pleasure to include it in this book, along with dozens of other true stories of Christmas—stories of real people who find joy in the midst of all kinds of circumstances.

As I searched the Bible for passages to follow each piece, I sought verses that will help the stories' messages overflow into our daily lives. I pray you will be inspired by these stories and Scriptures in the midst of an often harried season.

True joy is found when we strip Christmas down to its essence: Love, hope, and peace are found in God and in his Son. This gift is ours every day of the year. As the little boy in the story "Christmas Is . . ." reminds us, "Christmas is the love of God shining through the darkness." May we always seek that shining love—a love that is calm and bright.

CHERYL KIRKING

ACKNOWLEDGMENTS

Special thanks to

my husband, David Kilker, and children Bryce,
Blake, and Sarah Jean, for recognizing that
when Mom writes a book, it's a family
project! I love you.

family and friends who have offered encouragement.

my agent, Chip MacGregor.

my editors, Jeanette Thomason, Mary Wenger,
and Fiona Soltes, along with the good folks at
Revell and Baker.

the wonderful writers who contributed their
stories.

you, the reader. I am grateful for the privilege of
sharing these pages with you.

'ROUND YON VIRGIN MOTHER AND CHILD

The Living Nativity

*Today in the town of David
a Savior has been born to you;
he is Christ the Lord.*

Luke 2:11

Choirs Still Singing, Glories Still Streaming

Bill Egan

Two young men, a 26-year-old assistant priest and a 31-year-old schoolteacher, quietly stood in front of the main altar at St. Nicholas Church on December 24, 1818. They watched villagers shuffle in from the darkness and winter's chill that had crept over Oberndorf along the Salzach River, eleven miles from the city of Salzburg. By the golden glow of candlelight, they prepared to celebrate midnight mass.

Just hours earlier the young priest, Joseph Mohr, had journeyed to the neighboring home of schoolmaster Franz Gruber, also the organist for St. Nicholas Church. Mohr brought along a poem he had written two years earlier while on assignment to a pilgrimage church in Mariapfarr, Austria. The priest had a special request of his musician friend: Would he compose a melody and accompaniment for two singers, choir, and guitar for his poem?

Whether the request came as an improvised solution to a breakdown of the St. Nicholas aged organ, or as Mohr's desire for something special for his parishioners at Christmas, no one knows. However, Gruber worked through the day on a composition and had it ready for the midnight mass.

As the congregation sat in hushed reverence Joseph Mohr and Franz Gruber began to sing the gentle harmonies backed by Mohr's guitar. The choir joined them to repeat the last two lines of each verse.

> Silent night, holy night,
> All is calm, all is bright,
> 'Round yon Virgin mother and child,
> Holy infant, so tender and mild,
> Sleep in heavenly peace,
> Sleep in heavenly peace.

> Silent night, holy night,
> Shepherds quake at the sight,
> Glories stream from heaven afar
> Heav'nly hosts sing alleluia
> Christ the Savior is born,
> Christ the Savior is born.

The worshiping congregation soaked in the words: "calm . . . bright . . . tender . . . mild . . . heavenly peace." The lyrics were carried by the soothing strains that floated high, then dipped to a humming, lulling low. An enchanting new carol rang through the church on that long-ago Christmas, but it wasn't too long before it moved beyond the walls of St. Nicholas in Oberndorf.

Glories indeed stream from heaven, two traveling families of Ziller Valley folksingers must have thought when they first heard the song. During subsequent years, the Rainer family didn't merely ponder the beauty of *"Stille Nacht,"* or "Silent Night." They worked the beautiful carol into their repertoire, singing it for one audience that included Emperor Franz I of Austria and Tsar Alexander I of Russia—and apparently for the first time in America at the Alexander Hamilton Monument in 1839 outside Trinity Church in New York City.

Meanwhile other folk groups from the Ziller Valley in the mountains of Austria's Tyrol began singing "Silent Night" as they performed all over Europe for nobles and wealthy patricians. Along the way, the song became known only as "the Tyrolian folk carol," while others called it "The Song from Heaven."

By the time "Silent Night" was known throughout Europe and the Americas, Joseph Mohr, who was born into poverty in 1792, had died penniless in 1848, and Gruber, the composer, was unknown outside his home area. In fact, some arrangers assumed "Silent Night" started as a melody by Haydn, Mozart, or even Beethoven.

More than a century later, in 1994, the discovery of a long lost arrangement of the carol from the hand of Joseph Mohr set aside all doubts about the composer, since the priest had penned in the upper right hand corner "Melodie von Xav. Gruber."

Perhaps these facts and discoveries are all part of what we could call the miracle of "Silent Night." For how could a humble priest know that his six-stanza poem would inspire folksingers, royalty, and foreign nations? Or that it would be translated into hundreds of languages around the world? How could a musician, barely known outside his own village, predict his simple composition would be carried across the Alps to small churches in New Zealand, great cathedrals in Rome, and enjoyed in homes around the globe every December for nearly two hundred years? And who could know that God would come to us as a poor baby lying in a manger?

And my spirit rejoices in God my Savior, for he has been mindful of the humble state of his servant. From now on all generations will call me blessed.

LUKE 1:47-48

THE MYSTERIOUS MOVING NATIVITY

Cheryl Kirking

MY FIVE-YEAR-OLD TRIPLETS watched intently as I carefully unwrapped the porcelain figures of the nativity set.

"Can we help, Mama?" Sarah Jean asked hopefully.

"I think I'll do it this year, honey," I answered. "But you can set up your crèche today," I suggested, reminding them of the molded plastic nativity set they had been given. They inched in closer. "I like this one better," Bryce remarked. "Me too," Blake agreed. "They look more real."

I arranged the figures on a piece of green velvet, as I do every year. In the center lay baby Jesus in the manger, with Mary and Joseph on each side. Keeping a respectful distance is the shepherd, his lamb resting dutifully at his feet. The wise men approach from one side, as if arriving from their long journey.

The next morning I noticed that all the figures were clustered in a tight circle around the manger. So I put them all back in their proper places. By afternoon they were all packed in that little circle again. Once again, I returned them to their original places, only to find them a couple hours later, tightly gathered around the manger! Even the lamb's head was resting right on baby Jesus' foot. I glanced across the room at the children's nativity. There too, the wise men, shepherds, cattle, and all crowded the Christ child in a tight circle. Obviously, one or more of my little rascals was rearranging my nativity set! I felt a tiny flash of irritation before experiencing a far greater flash of inspiration.

Isn't this what Christmas is all about, drawing as close as we possibly can to Christ?

I smiled and began to quietly sing:

> *O come, let us adore him,*
> *O come, let us adore him,*
> *O come, let us adore him,*
> *Christ, the Lord!*

Let the little children come to me, and do not hinder them, for the kingdom of God belongs to such as these.

MARK 10:14

WHAT DOES JOE DO?

Louisa Godissart McQuillen

THE NIGHT OF NOVEMBER 18TH was cold and snowy. It was also my daughter Erin's birthday. To celebrate, her husband, Tim, took her to the Penn State–Notre Dame football game in nearby Beaver Stadium. But I received a present, too: I got to babysit my little grandson, J.P., aged three. After his parents left, J.P. and I bundled up in warm coats and went out to do some "Christmas looking."

Eventually we found ourselves in front of Philipsburg's True Value Hardware, gazing at an almost life-sized nativity display in the store's showcase window. Mary, Joseph, and the Christ child looked almost real enough to speak.

I think the life-like figures overwhelmed J.P., who had seen only miniature versions of the familiar Christmas scene. Looking bewildered, he stared at the babe a moment, and then started firing questions at me:

"Who's that, Nanny?"

I leaned down so I could look him in the eye. "Why, that's baby Jesus, J.P.," I answered. "You've seen the nativity scene before. Don't you remember?"

He looked at the figures again, this time at the babe's mother kneeling before the manger. "Who's that one?"

I smiled. "That's Mary, Jesus' mother," I explained, watching him with amusement. J.P. looked higher, his eyes pausing on the staunch-looking figure with a bearded face. His eyes then traveled downward, past the man's walking staff and on down to his sandaled feet. But J.P. said nothing more. He just stood there looking, his nose bright pink from the cold, mittened hands down at his sides.

In a typically childish manner, the little guy was "observing" on his own. Yet he was quiet for so long, that I decided to prompt him. "And that's Joseph, Jesus' father!" I added. J.P. seemed even more thoughtful as he stared at the tall figure standing so protectively over his little family.

Suddenly he asked, "What does Joe do?"

"What?" I asked, startled at his informal naming of Mary's husband. I wasn't sure I had even heard him right! "What?" I dumbly repeated. He asked again, "What does Joe do, Nanny?" I laughed, but J.P. was serious. He wanted to know more.

Perhaps J.P. was comparing Jesus' daddy with his own. J.P.'s daddy, however, wears a gun and holster at his side, not a hiking staff. Tim is a Pennsylvania state policeman, whose tall black boots and gray uniform must have seemed far removed from Joseph's flowing robes and sandaled feet!

I thought about the words that sprang from an inquisitive three-year-old's heart: "What does Joe do, Nanny?" I knew that God chose Joseph to be his Son's earthly stepfather, yet I wondered if this explanation might be hard for a three-year-old child to grasp. So I told J.P. in simple terms how "Joe" had fit into the Christmas story.

His question was as old as Mary and Joseph themselves—and perhaps as confusing back then as it was to J.P. on this snowy, wintry night. Besides the fact that family lineage gave him proper credentials, just what did Joe *do?*

Could it be that simple *obedience* was Joseph's greatest attribute? He could have ignored the voice urging him to marry the young girl. He also could have talked himself out of the marriage, since friends probably questioned his sanity in even considering it. Rumors, you know, indicated Mary was already with child.

What would we have said if Joseph was our friend and told us his intended wife carried another's child? No doubt, they said it, too: "Surely you jest, Joe! Wake up and smell the coffee, man!"

Perhaps Joseph's own mind mocked him. How could Mary be a virgin? Even so, he did as the angel requested and he married her. Obeying fully, "he had no union with her until she gave birth to a son" (Matt. 1:25). And Joseph was so tuned in to God's voice that he sensed imminent danger. He rushed his little family into Egypt, where they lived until it was safe to return home.

Time after time, Joseph followed God's leading, straight and true, like an arrow follows a path from the bow that releases it. In fact, that's how I answered J.P.'s question: "What does Joe do, J.P.? He obeys God. Joe's like a straight arrow that flies where the bow directs it. And all of us should try to be more like him!"

My answer must have satisfied the little guy. He stuffed one hand deep in his jacket pocket. With the other, he led me into the warmth of the store to look at toys.

> *This is love: that we walk in obedience to his commands. As you have heard from the beginning, his command is that you walk in love.*
>
> 2 JOHN 6

Manger Babies

Linda LaMar Jewell

WHEN MY OLDER SISTER, Jannet, was seven, I was five, and my younger sister, Sharon, was eighteen months old, Grandma took us with her when she milked two cows, Old Blue and Red Spot. In the barn, Grandma filled the three smooth, wooden feed boxes with sweet-smelling native hay.

At milking time, Grandma first wrapped my baby sister in a soft, pink afghan, then again in a durable woolen army blanket and laid her in the manger closest to her. Before sitting down to milk the cow, Grandma took Jannet and me by the hands and led us to a place where we would be safe, while warning us to stay clear of the cow's hooves. We heeded Grandma's caution and "stayed put" while she milked the big, blue roan and the red Guernsey. Sitting on a three-legged stool, Grandma was a bulwark of safety between us and the towering milk cows.

Besides Grandma's occasional "Whoa, now," the only barn sounds were the crunch of the cows eating

27

hay, the swish of their tails, and the rhythmic pings of milk hitting the bottom of the metal pail before changing into foamy gurgles.

Afraid of the large milk cows, I didn't budge. Grandma's warnings were unnecessary. Glad for her presence, I clutched Jannet's hand, and with wide eyes, I watched luminous hay motes slowly swirl in patterned shafts of sunlight before disappearing into gloomy recesses of the earthy-smelling barn.

Turning my head to follow the sunbeams to their source, I beheld the radiance from a small window that illuminated the manger. My sleeping baby sister was much nearer the huge milk cow than I was. Yet Sharon's peaceful repose dispelled my fears.

I picture baby Jesus looking a lot like Sharon, only newer and smaller, wrapped in blankets, lying on the sweet-smelling native hay. The serene image of my baby sister sleeping in the manger while the cows were feeding so close by reminds me of God Almighty's protection and peace. I, too, can rest securely in the Lord because of another baby who slept in a manger more than two thousand years ago. "This shall be a sign unto you; Ye shall find the babe wrapped in swaddling clothes, lying in a manger" (Luke 2:12 KJV).

When I feel surrounded by gloom and afraid of situations larger than I am, I'm grateful that the manger scene reminds me that the Lord is God Almighty, bigger than my fears. For when I feel small and helpless in the presence of danger, I remember that, like Grandma looking after her granddaughters' safety at milking time, God also is a bulwark between us and our fears. With loving hands, he wraps his children

in his protection and puts us in a secure place while
he goes about his work.

> *I will lie down and sleep in peace, for
> you alone, O LORD, make me dwell in
> safety.*
>
> PSALM 4:8

The Good Shepherd

Brenda Nixon

"Out of the mouths of babes" comes discerning truth. As a young mother, this adage held special meaning one Christmas when I was in despair amid the holiday stress. With cards to mail, plays to rehearse, clothes to wash, a house to clean, food to buy, devotions to have, parents to call, baths to give, I nearly collapsed. The haste of the holidays was too much. Added to that, my husband's job was shaky and the grim thought of no income had me depressed.

Among my numerous responsibilities was teaching my three-year-old's Sunday school class at church. I found teaching the class a delight and a time I usually looked forward to. But on this particular day, I had to muster energy just to prepare for it. With other demands bearing down on me, I grabbed a cup of coffee and collected my notes. Following a deep sigh, I began perusing the teacher's book. "What! The Good Shepherd?" I complained. "Surely something is wrong here. How does the Good Shepherd relate to the real meaning of Christmas? Besides, city kids can't relate to a shepherd," I argued. My low spirit was evident as I criticized everything about this lesson.

Each time I read a paragraph, my mind went to other burdens. How would we survive if my husband lost his job? How can we pay for my older child's braces? Why does our car stall at intersections? I still need to wrap the kids' gifts. I can't do this alone. I need help! But then, my thoughts returned to the page. I wanted to help these precious minds learn that God is like a good shepherd. Not just a shepherd but a "good" one. "What makes a good shepherd?" would be my key question. "Lord, help me to find something meaningful to share with these precious preschoolers," I prayed. Little did I know that he had something indeed—but it was for me.

Sunday arrived. I gathered my lesson materials, whispered another prayer, and, still feeling a bit depressed, attempted a smile. After settling my older one in her room, my daughter and I hustled into the class for three year olds. We listened to music while I took attendance. The children looked so cute in their green velvet dresses and red bow ties on crisp white shirts. We survived the art portion of the lesson, gluing cotton balls to sheep pictures, and had our juice and animal crackers. Then it was circle time. Turning to each rosy-cheeked cherub, I began with, "What is a 'good' shepherd?" To which came my reminder of truth as one tot positively replied, "He picks up his sheep when they fall down."

He tends his flock like a shepherd:
He gathers the lambs in his arms
and carries them close to his heart;
he gently leads those that have
young.

ISAIAH 40:11

WHERE'S THE BABY JESUS?

Jeannie S. Williams

A NATIVITY SCENE without the baby Jesus?!
I have one proudly displayed at home each Christmas. For me, it's a reminder of a past holiday when I purchased the broken set.

I was bitter and disheartened that year because my parents, after thirty-six years of marriage, were getting a divorce. I could not accept their decision to part, and I became depressed, not realizing they needed my love and understanding more than ever.

My thoughts were constantly filled with childhood memories—the huge Christmas trees, the gleaming decorations, the special gifts, and the love we shared as a close family. Every time I'd think about those moments, I'd burst into tears, sure I'd never feel the spirit of Christmas again. But for my children's sake, I decided to make the effort, joining the last-minute shoppers.

They pushed, shoved, and complained as they grabbed from shelves and racks. Christmas tree lights

33

and ornaments dangled from open boxes, and the few dolls and stuffed toys sitting on the nearly emptied shelves reminded me of neglected orphans. A small nativity scene had fallen to the floor in front of my shopping cart, and I stopped to put it back on the shelf.

After glancing at the endless checkout line, I decided it wasn't worth the effort and had made up my mind to leave when suddenly I heard a loud, sharp voice cry out.

"Sarah! You get that thing out of your mouth right now 'fore I slap you!"

"But Mommy! I wasn't puttin' it in my mouth! See, Mommy? I was kissin' it! Look, Mommy, it's a little baby Jesus!"

"Well I don't care what it is! You put it down right now! You hear me?"

"But come look, Mommy," the child insisted. "It's all broken. It's a little manger and the baby Jesus got broked off."

As I listened from the next aisle, I found myself smiling and wanting to see the little girl who had kissed the baby Jesus.

She appeared to be about four or five years old and was not properly dressed for the cold, wet weather. Bright, colorful pieces of yarn were tied on the ends of her braids, making her look cheerful despite her ragged attire.

Reluctantly, I turned my eyes to her mother. She was paying no attention to the child but was anxiously looking through the marked-down winter coats on the bargain rack. She was also shabbily dressed, and her torn, dirty tennis shoes were wet from the cold, melting snow. Asleep in her shopping cart was a small baby bundled snugly in a thick, washed-out yellow blanket.

"Mommy!" the little girl called to her. "Can we buy this here little baby Jesus? We can set him on the table by the couch and we could . . ."

"I told you to put that thing down!" her mother interrupted. "You get yourself over here right now or I'm gonna give you a spankin'! You hear me?"

Angrily, the woman hurried toward the child. I turned away, not wanting to watch, expecting her to punish the child as she had threatened. A few seconds passed.

No movement, no scolding. Just complete silence. Puzzled, I peeked again and was astonished to see the mother kneeling on the wet, dirty floor holding the child close to her trembling body. She struggled to say something, but only managed a desperate sob.

"Don't cry, Mommy!" the child pleaded. Wrapping her arms around her mother, she apologized for her behavior. "I'm sorry I wasn't good in this store. I promise I won't ask for nothin' else! I don't want this here baby Jesus. Really I don't. See, I'll put him back here in the manger. Please don't cry no more, Mommy!"

"I'm sorry too, honey!" answered her mother finally. "You know I don't have enough money to buy anything extra right now, and I'm just crying 'cause I wished I did—it being Christmas and all—but I bet come Christmas mornin', if you promise to be a real good girl, you just might find them pretty little play dishes you been wantin'—and maybe next year we can get us a real Christmas tree. How about that?"

"You know what, Mommy?" the child asked excitedly. "I don't really need this here little baby Jesus doll anyhow! You know why? 'Cause my Sunday school teacher says Jesus really lives in your heart! I'm glad he lives in my heart, aren't you, Mommy?"

I watched the child take her mother's hand and walk to the front of the store. Her simple words, exclaimed with excitement, were echoing through my mind: "He lives in my heart."

I looked at the nativity scene and realized that a baby born in a stable some two thousand years ago is a person who still walks with us today, making his presence known, working to bring us through the difficulties of life, if only we will let him.

"Thank you, God," I began to pray. "Thank you for a wonderful childhood filled with precious memories, and for parents who provided a home for me and gave me the love I needed during the most important years of my life. But most of all, thank you for giving us your Son."

Quickly, I grabbed the various pieces of the nativity scene and hurried to the check-out counter to pay for it. Recognizing one of the clerks, I asked her to give the doll to the little girl who was then leaving the store with her mother. I watched the child accept the gift and then give baby Jesus another kiss as she walked out the door.

The little broken nativity scene reminds me every year of a child whose simple words touched my life—and transformed my despair into new assurance and joy.

The baby Jesus is not there, of course, but every time I look at the empty manger I know I can answer the question, "Where's the baby Jesus?"

He's in my heart!

I pray that out of his glorious riches he may strengthen you with power through his Spirit in your inner being, so that Christ may dwell in your hearts through faith.

EPHESIANS 3:16–17

SLEEP
IN HEAVENLY
PEACE

Tranquility Restored

I heard the bells on Christmas Day
Their old, familiar carols play,
And wild and sweet the words repeat
Of peace on earth, good will to men!

HENRY WADSWORTH LONGFELLOW

THE BRACELET PROMISE

Carmen Leal

THE GLITTER OF GREEN STONES drew me to the solitary display case. The light bounced off the silver and glass. Amid the jumble of holiday shoppers, I made my way to the corner area reserved for fine jewelry and gazed upon the bracelet, noticing the unique handiwork. The beaten silver, fashioned in such a way as to resemble diamond chips, was delightful. Seeing dozens of dark green emeralds, I knew this was a one-of-a-kind treasure.

As I stared in wonder at the intricate piece, I remembered a promise my husband had made. David had bought me a lovely gift four years before on our honeymoon. He had selected an emerald green Austrian crystal-and-seed-pearl bracelet in honor of my May birthstone. As he fastened it on my wrist, he lovingly said, "I promise you that soon I will buy you real emeralds. Just wait." Though I loved the honeymoon gift, deep down I looked forward to David's promise.

Until that time, however, I still delighted in wearing the delicate creation. I wore it frequently, each time remembering the island boutique where he found it. Whenever David saw the bracelet, he remembered his promise, and would reassure me that the time he would keep it was coming soon.

It became our habit over the years to look in every jewelry store window as if searching for the Holy Grail. We wandered in and out of countless shops, becoming discouraged when we realized that the cost of the promise was well beyond our means. I soon wavered in my belief that I would ever own what David desired to give me. But David never lost faith.

Now it was the last week before Christmas, and we were in the mall to buy gifts for our children. Finances were tight; we had agreed there would be no exchange of gifts between us. We had just completed one of the most stressful years possible. With David's diagnosis of Huntington's disease, our lives had forever changed. This terminal, neurological disorder had pitched us into a panic, not to mention near-bankruptcy.

I looked up from the case into David's eyes and saw love shining even brighter than the stones. I could tell in his mind that nothing short of this bracelet would satisfy his honeymoon promise, but I knew there was no way we could possibly afford it. I tried to tell him, but the words died on my lips. He'd had so many disappointments this year, I didn't have the heart to tell him the answer was no.

Thinking fast, I came up with a reason to decline what I knew was an offer I could not accept. I have large wrists and normally bracelets don't fit. As the store clerk reverently lifted the object out of the case, I knew it would be too small.

The silver and green made a colorful contrast against my brown skin. I silently acknowledged how much I wanted this bracelet while hoping it would not fit. As the clerk reached around my wrist and closed the intricate clasp, my heart both plummeted and leapt. It fit! It was perfect, yet I knew there was no way we could afford it. The unpaid bills, with more looming in the future, had placed a vise around our checkbook.

I glanced at my best friend and saw his shining smile burst forth. This man, who had never hurt anyone, was now the victim of one of the cruelest diseases known to man. His was a sentence with only one verdict: Death. Untimely, slow, and cruel death. My eyes brimmed with tears as I realized we would not live out our dream of growing old together. To David, this was not just one more bauble in an already overcrowded jewelry box. Rather, this was his love displayed on my arm for all the world to see. To David, a promise made was a promise to be kept. I sadly realized that he might not have many more months or years to keep his promise. Suddenly it became the most important covenant ever made. Somehow I had to juggle the bills to let him have the honor of keeping his promise.

"Do you like it?" he whispered. Hearing the hope in his voice, mingled with seeing the love in his eyes, was something I am sure few women ever have the privilege of experiencing. It was clear that David cherished me. All he ever wanted, from the day we met, was to please me.

"Yes, honey, I love it." I answered. "It's exactly what I want."

The clerk reached for my arm to remove the brace-let. I could not believe this little object had worked its way into my heart so quickly. "How much is it?" I finally asked.

Slowly the man turned over the little white tag. Two hundred fifty dollars. Surely it was a mistake! I had seen enough to know that price was only a fraction of its worth.

The man began to extol the virtues of the item, pointing out the one hundred and eighty emeralds in a handmade Brazilian setting. But even though two hundred fifty dollars was an incredible price, it might as well have been twenty-five hundred dollars for all we could stretch our meager budget. Without thinking, I asked, "Would you take two hundred twenty-five dollars, tax included?" I surprised myself at the question since shops in malls do not normally bargain. He looked at me in surprise, but answered, "That will be fine."

Before he could change his mind, I whipped out my credit card, all the while watching as David beamed with pride. The man quickly handled the transaction and we were on our way. Every few steps we would stop and look at the bracelet. Before we reached the car, David said, "When I get sicker and eventually die, you need to look at each emerald. Each one will remind you of something special we've done. A trip we took, a movie we saw, or a moment we shared. This will be your memory bracelet." I began to cry. David's concern was not his own failing health, but for how I would handle life without him.

As we worked our way home in the bumper-to-bumper traffic in rush-hour Honolulu, I wondered just how we could pay for the bracelet. Oddly enough, I never really panicked. I was just curious to see how it would all work out. We talked as we traveled and every so often, looked at the miracle of the promise kept.

On the way into the house I grabbed the mail and began to open it. Amid the usual bills were two cards. I opened the first, which was from a church where I had sung several times that year. It was a thank-you note for my music ministry, along with a gift. I was speechless. I was looking at a check for two hundred dollars! I reached for the second card and slit it open. Out fell two bills: a twenty and a five. The card was simply signed, "A friend in Christ."

I looked up at David and we both began to laugh. I remembered how I had felt the need to ask the clerk if he would take two hundred twenty-five dollars, tax included. Even as we were in the mall, the payment for David's promise was in the mailbox. God had already taken care of every detail.

It is just a piece of jewelry, something I could have lived without. But the memories attached to our time together have helped make me the woman I am today. The exquisite joy and the unspeakable grief of this relationship have matured me in ways I never could have anticipated. The promise David spoke on our honeymoon had been fulfilled. It was only through God that we stopped at that shop on that day to find that specific bracelet. And only through him that the pastor of a small church, coupled with an unknown friend, knew the best gifts to give.

Before I was ever born, God made another promise. He promised me eternal salvation. He promised he would be with me every step of the way. All I had to do was ask. Just as God never stopped believing I would claim that first promise, David never stopped believing in his bracelet promise. And now, when I wear my emeralds, I pull out memories I keep tucked away in my heart—those of David's faith as well as God's promises.

Let us hold unswervingly to the hope
we profess, for he who promised is
faithful.

HEBREWS 10:23

FULL CIRCLE

Raymond Flagg Jr.

THERE WERE TIMES while teaching that I found myself wondering if the activity in progress was worth all the effort. My course on homesteading showed students how to take practical advantage of natural resources found on their land. But I often asked myself, "Is this project something for which the students will ever have a real, practical use?"

At that time, communities around our school district had a 16.5 percent unemployment rate, with projections of a tough New England winter. Times were hard for many of my students' families.

On the day school reconvened after Christmas break, however, a student approached my desk. "Teacher, I want you to know, thanks to you, my family had the best Christmas ever."

Surprised at his unexpected statement, I asked, "How did I help?"

"Well, my father hurt his back where he works. Money has been pretty scarce. I took home that wreath you showed us how to make. We was all sitting around the kitchen table looking it over. Mother said she thought we ought to be able to sell some wreaths to get Christmas money. She said, 'Go get those extra coat hangers in the closets.' My father knew there was some wire in the shop almost like what we used and we had plenty of fir brush growing on our land. Us five kids all went off to gather up supplies. I showed them how to cut the brush and wire it to the coat hanger ring.

"We made fifty wreaths and tied them on top of the station wagon. Mother found enough stuff to decorate one real pretty. All of us climbed into the car and headed for Augusta. We parked in that big parking lot at the mall and put up our cardboard sign. We sold the first one in nothing flat! Mother took that money and went into the store and bought decorations. We sold every wreath as fast as she and I could decorate them. We got five whole dollars apiece for the rest of 'em!

"Well, we divvied up the money between us and went shopping. Boy, it was fun to see my brothers and sisters learning to make those wreaths and then shopping with the money they got for selling them.

"My folks wanted me to say thanks, Teacher. You really helped us out."

I thanked him and patted him on the back as I turned away so he wouldn't see my tears. My joy in teaching had come back to me full circle—like the circle of those wreaths.

*For the LORD your God will bless you
in all your harvest and in all the work
of your hands, and your joy will
be complete.*

DEUTERONOMY 16:15

GOODWILL ON EARTH

Judy Ann Squier

SPEEDING UP TO THE GOODWILL collection truck, I
felt anything but ready for Christmas. I had cleaned
closets and cupboards to make room for the deluge
of Christmas gifts one week away.

Glancing at my watch, I realized I was out of time,
with my dentist appointment in fifteen minutes across
town. "This will take only thirty seconds," I spoke
out loud, trying to steady my harried nerves.

"Hurray for a clean house!" I cheered as the car
in front of me moved out of my way.

A cordial attendant met me at the rear of my mini-
van. Swinging open the hatchback, we were greeted
by a tumble of used clothes, dolls, shoes, belts, towels,
and a burlap lamp shade. "I want to keep this con-
tainer," I spoke hurriedly, pointing to my four-foot-
long plastic bin. "I'll need about ten bags."

"I'm out of bags," said the dark-haired girl, looking
down at the faded blacktop.

Irritation joined my frustration. I held my tongue, tempted to declare, "I did not come here to fail. This stuff is going on the ground."

Sensing my fury, the shy attendant said nervously, "I can't take your stuff without containers. My truck goes to the warehouse today and I'd get in trouble if it arrived a mess."

Rubbing her hands, the young woman stood trapped between her job's requirements and her customer's demands. I tottered between total body collapse and imposing my "rights," feeling more kinship with a volcano ready to blow than a Christian homemaker preparing to celebrate God Incarnate.

And that's when it happened. Suddenly, the Spirit took over.

"I'll get some bags over there," I heard myself volunteer, pointing to the grocery store fifty feet across the parking lot. "Do you want a drink?" I offered. My words caught us both off guard.

"No, thanks," she answered as I took off.

Composed, but on a mission, I entered the market heading toward the nearest idle checkstand. "May I take these?" I asked, reaching for a dozen brown bags.

"Sure, they're yours," smiled the busy bag boy two aisles over.

In a flash I was back at the truck, triumphant. Visibly relieved, the attendant joined me behind my car. Side by side we worked. She held the bag, I filled. Eight bags all together.

I said, "Thank you. God bless." She replied, "Merry Christmas!" as I got into my car and drove off. That was it. Neither of us could tell what had made a good day out of a bad scene, but together we could tell the exact moment grace appeared. In tandem, we had experienced "peace on earth, goodwill toward men." Taking a final peek in my rearview mirror, I savored the gift of not only my cleaner house, but also my cleaner heart.

He who seeks good finds goodwill.
PROVERBS 11:27

MYSTERY GUEST

James A. McClung

IT WAS NOVEMBER 1975 when my father-in-law had
his first heart attack. My wife, Betty, and I felt she
should be with her mother in Norfolk, Virginia, during his time of recuperation. We decided we would
drive to spend Thanksgiving dinner at her parents'
home, and Betty would stay behind. So I bundled up
our five-year-old twins, Walt and Tondra, and headed
back to Richmond. Leaving Betty was difficult, but I
was sure I could handle everything.

Little did I know that, while she was gone, little
Walt would develop a medical problem. I took Walt
to the doctor three times, and after each time he'd
feel better—before feeling worse again. I decided
he needed his Mama, so we drove to get Betty and
brought her home.

I had downplayed Walt's situation, knowing that
Betty had enough on her mind at the time. To ease
the mood, Tondra and Walt had gone with me to a
florist, where we bought a Norfolk Pine and decorated

it. We affixed a tag on it that read, "While you were in Norfolk, we were pining for you." Betty was delighted when she saw it—a little joy for a change. It was short-lived, however, because Walt became ill again. I was determined to find out what was wrong.

The doctor told us that there was a mass in Walt's right side, and sent us to a surgeon. Within a day, Walt was in surgery for kidney problems. The surgeon told us after surgery that "everything will be all right—unless he has a twin." Tondra, it turned out, had the same congenital kidney defect, and was immediately hospitalized for the same surgery.

That Christmas Eve night, as we were readying the children for bed, I looked over to see my son with a tube coming out of his side, thinking of the second surgery that was to follow—another tube out the other side. I looked at my wife, sitting in her chair with dark circles around her eyes. She looked like a raccoon. She had been keeping so much emotion bottled up inside.

My daughter was in the other bed, anticipating her surgery. Everyone was asleep. Suddenly, I felt very alone. As a pastor, I felt I should have had faith enough to spare, but going through this pain with my wife and children, I was lost. I tried in vain to summon up Scripture for consolation—it seemed as though the well I had drawn upon so many times to comfort others had gone dry for me. I started crying, quietly so as not to wake anyone, and must have cried myself to sleep. I remember praying, "God, I really need to know you're with me in this. You gave us such a special child in your Son, Jesus, and I need to feel your presence somehow. Amen."

At approximately 6:00 A.M., there was a knock at the door that woke Betty and me. I went to the door to find Santa Claus standing there! He didn't have a fake beard—he looked just like Santa should look. He came into the room, waking the children by calling their names. Their faces lit up with joy! After giving them each a gift, he said, "Now I have to get back to the North Pole—I've had a long night!" Without another word, he left, but the joy he brought lingered in the room as the children opened their presents.

I wanted to go thank him, but Santa was nowhere to be found. When I asked the nurses if they had seen Santa Claus, one said, "Mister, there has been no one here but us!" Had it been a dream? It couldn't have been. My wife and children had seen Santa too! "But he was just here," I insisted. "Didn't you see him?" No one had seen him, nor could anyone offer an explanation of how he got into the hospital.

I passed by the hospital chapel and breathed a prayer of gratitude. I knew that God had heard my prayer, and answered it with a Christmas miracle.

My children are now grown and married. But they—and I—still believe in Santa Claus. God sent him to us that Christmas morning.

The LORD bless you and keep you;
the LORD make his face shine upon
you and be gracious to you; the LORD
turn his face toward you and give you
peace.

NUMBERS 6:24–26

SEASON OF LOVE

Irene Bastian

THE WEARY YOUNG WOMAN lined up several card-board boxes and tenderly packed each with socks, underclothes, and clean, mended outfits. The oldest and youngest children would stay with her. The next two, a boy and a girl, would go to their paternal grandparents. The middle child would stay on an aunt's farm, and the remaining two girls would be cared for by her parents.

She and her husband had finally found a suite in an older home within the city. The basement was rented out in three sections. Two other families shared the space and all had access to one bathroom and the laundry facilities, but there just wasn't room for all seven children. There was no other choice. It was the only place they could afford. She prayed it wouldn't be for long and that soon, things would be easier.

The children excitedly clamored into waiting cars to embark on their new adventures. Waving good-byes, they didn't see the tears or pain in their mother's face or hear her cry to God as her hands clutched her swelling abdomen. "O Lord, I can't even take care of them. How will I be able to care for another one?"

That young woman was my mother, and I, the middle child. I was too young to realize the hard times my parents were facing, but as weeks turned into months, I longed for my family.

One snowy evening, my aunt drove me to my maternal grandparents' home. It was Christmas Eve, and Mom, Dad, my brother, and all my sisters were there. What a commotion! A cardboard carton with Kellogg's Corn Flakes printed on the side was tucked in beside a chair in the corner. Sweet cooing sounds emerged from it. I approached the makeshift bassinet and for the first time gazed upon my beautiful baby sister. She reminded me of the baby in the nativity scene outside the church. People had gathered around beholding baby Jesus lying in a wooden box. Now I had my own special baby in a box! I felt our family was special.

Before long, we were scurried off to bed. Four of us found our spots in one bed by alternating heads and feet. Giggles, tales of what was happening in our lives, talk of baby Jesus and Santa Claus kept us awake for hours. It was good to be a family together again. We were content.

Christmas morning brought us scrambling to the tree to see if there were any gifts. For me, there was the most beautiful doll I would ever own. She had a wooden head with blue eyes that opened and closed and a cloth body attached to wooden arms and legs. She had some scuffs on her face and some of her toes and fingers were chipped, but she was *mine*. I tenderly kissed her wounds.

Cousins began to arrive. The smell of turkey roasting and other festive goodies filtered through the air. We packed ourselves into an old church pew that served as a bench behind the table and shared Christmas dinner. Unfortunately, all too soon it was over, and once again, we went our separate ways with promises we would be together again soon. At least now I had my Janet doll to love.

I later learned that the city's firefighters knew of my parents' plight. The toys we received were used toys citizens had donated for firefighters to repair and distribute to needy families. They helped make my Christmas unforgettable.

By the time Christmas rolled around again, my family had been reunited. Things were not always easy, but we were together. As we grew, we saw our parents extending help to other families in need, giving even though it made things tighter for them. We children would scamper off to find a jacket, shoes, sweater, outfit, or toy that some other child might treasure. Mom filled boxes with preserves, carrots, potatoes, and even home-raised chicken. Dad inspected our offerings and packed them into the station wagon. For we knew, through the kindness of others—family, friends, and even people we didn't know—love is truly about unselfish giving.

A new command I give to you: Love one another. As I have loved you, so you must love one another. By this all men will know that you are my disciples, if you love one another.

JOHN 13:34–35

CHRISTMAS
OF MY DREAMS

Cheryl Kirking

"WE HAVE GOT TO GET this house cleaned by Christmas!" I declared to my husband. Dave looked up from the bills he was paying, glanced around the kitchen, and asked wryly, "*This* Christmas?" I too scanned the cluttered room. Play-Doh animals were drying on the counter, "ABC" magnets were stuck not only to the refrigerator, but also to most of the kitchen chair legs. A zoo of stuffed animals had occupied one corner of the adjacent family room for over a week. A castle of large cardboard blocks threatened to topple over in another corner. Stacks of picture books were piled on the coffee table. Our triplets were three years old, and it showed! I sighed as I slumped down on the wear-worn couch.

"At least we didn't have to put a fence around the Christmas tree this year!" Dave offered. I smiled, remembering the various ways we tried to keep our past trees triplet-proof, including suspending it from the ceiling. "That's true," I agreed, surveying the towering Scotch pine. It was enormous, brushing the ceiling. The owner of the Christmas tree farm had said this would be his last year selling trees, so all the trees were the same price, regardless of size. Dave and I got caught up in the children's enthusiasm, and ended up cutting the biggest one we could find. The children had hung most of the ornaments on the bottom third of the tree, so the star on top looked mighty lonely.

Dave plugged in the tree lights and squeezed next to me on the couch, amid some animals that had escaped from the "zoo." We gazed at the tree, its bottom-heavy branches sagging. That afternoon I had tried to help the children make ornaments by covering cardboard stars with aluminum foil. They decided, however, that it was quicker to just ball up wads of foil and stick them in among the branches. They had used up the entire roll of foil making a couple dozen of these unusual ornaments.

"I actually thought that this year I'd try out an idea I had seen in a magazine," I laughed. "I *was* going to weave gold ribbons throughout the branches, with sprigs of dried baby's breath."

"Uh . . . I don't think it's gonna happen this year!" Dave mused. "But you know what your dad would say," he said.

"I think this is the nicest tree we've ever had!" we both recited in unison. My dad says that every year about my parents' tree.

I sighed again, and snuggled closer to my husband. It *was* the nicest tree we'd ever had—foil wads and all.

Christmas of My Dreams

The Christmas cookies all are frosted,
the gingerbread men have purple hair.
And 'cause little hands can only reach so high,
the top half of the tree is quite bare!
But the bottom half sparkles with tinsel
and foil stars and paper chains,
And along with the gifts the Wise Men bring
are three nickels and two candy canes.

Although it's true our money's tighter than
    ever,
our love just keeps on growing, it seems.
And I couldn't ask for anything more;
this is the Christmas of my dreams.

I used to have such great expectations
about Christmas and just how it should be,
With the picture-perfect table of goodies
and lots of presents under the tree.
Although I still love the tinsel and glitter,
the scent of pine and songs in the air,
When all's said and done, what matters most
is the Christmas love that all of us share.

Although our Christmas may not be very fancy,
like the ones you see in magazines,
I wouldn't trade it for anything;
this is the Christmas of my dreams.

So let's each count our blessings,
and thank our God above,
As we celebrate this season
of the Greatest Gift of Love.

Our Christmas may not be very fancy,
like the ones you see in magazines,
But I couldn't ask for anything more;
this is the Christmas of my dreams.

1994 CHERYL KIRKING/MILL POND MUSIC

SLEEP
IN HEAVENLY
PEACE

62

Thanks be to God for his
indescribable gift!
2 CORINTHIANS 9:15

Chocolate-Covered Love

B. J. Taylor

THE FIRST YEAR without the familiar rectangular-shaped box under the Christmas tree was the hardest. The sweet, tantalizing, melt-in-your-mouth richness of a cherry surrounded by white cream, nestled in a cup of chocolate, is what made Christmas and all its traditions special for me. That, and the fact that chocolate-covered cherries were my dad's favorite.

Christmas morning held lots of suspense, with gift-opening put on hold until after the traditional breakfast of bacon, eggs, cinnamon rolls, and eggnog with nutmeg sprinkled on top. Everyone pitched in and helped, with one person frying the bacon, another stirring the eggs, and still another watching the rolls so they didn't burn.

After the dishes were washed and dried we'd all troop out to the living room to gather by the Christmas tree. As my brother handed out each festively wrapped gift, the mounds of presents grew in front of each recipient. The little kids were allowed to open theirs first, with mom and dad helping to tear off the paper and say the thank yous. But the bigger kids weren't allowed to open them all at once. They had to wait, like the rest of us, as we opened our gifts one by one.

The morning flew by. Breakfast had been hours before, and stomachs were now growling. No one wanted to stop, yet everyone needed a little pick-me-up.

"A little chocolate would do right about now," Aunt Millie was fond of saying. And she was right. Of all the gifts waiting to be opened, everyone hoped they'd see a box of something chocolate.

And then, there one was. Rectangular in shape, that familiar three-by-eight-inch box held the most prized of delights on this Christmas morning. They were chocolate, all right. Chocolate-covered cherries, to be exact. The perfect mid-morning Christmas snack.

The first year they appeared, they were gone in an instant. It was part of Christmas, after all, to share. One pass around the room and even the second layer was missing by the time it returned to its owner.

I knew my dad really liked them, so the next year I bought his favorite, milk chocolate, and wrapped them as a gift. That same year, he gave them to me, only dark chocolate, wrapped in bright red paper. When we opened them that morning we immediately passed them around, enjoying the oohs and aahs from all the family members as they bit into the side, licked out the cream, and munched on the cherry.

Today, I buy two boxes at Christmas, one milk chocolate and one dark. And even though Dad isn't here, his spirit lives on. Every Christmas day at mid-morning, we stop, pass around the boxes of chocolate-covered cherries, and remember Dad. It's with bittersweet emotions that I bite into my first one, savoring the memories of Christmas past and looking forward with delight to the sweetness of Christmas present and future.

I have not stopped giving thanks for you, remembering you in my prayers.

EPHESIANS 1:16

TEA LEAF CHRISTMAS

Mary Linn McClure

ONE SNOWY, BLUSTERY DAY, a few days before Christmas, my friend Debe and I decided to treat ourselves to a special day of antiquing. I had the holiday blues. My Christmas had not been the same since Mom's death; she was my best friend.

Memories of garage sales and various antique stores filled my mind. Mom and I went antiquing Saturday mornings during the spring and summer. We traveled the suburbs and surrounding towns. Each antique shop was quaint and dilapidated. Rusted farm tools leaned against peeling painted exteriors, but inside were treasures. The more junk, the better we liked it.

We concentrated on items Mom collected. She was always wanting to add to her Tea Leaf Ironstone collection of pottery. Tea Leaf was made in England around 1900. The pottery was simple but elegant, bluish white with a copper leaf design and a band of copper luster. Mom had about thirty pieces, but good pieces were hard to find.

After our treasure hunts, we always stopped for ice cream. Those were times when I learned about Mom's life as she told me about her childhood on a farm in Lancaster, Missouri, during the Depression. I can remember her telling me that the Lancaster town café used Tea Leaf dishes on their tables.

The copper inlay on the Tea Leaf reminded Mom of her mother's copper kettle, where applesauce was stirred over the fire. And when Mom died, I inherited her collection of Tea Leaf.

As Debe and I approached the store that day in December, I ran ahead. The door creaked as we opened it. Inside we could smell hot apple cider and freshly brewed coffee. Dusty relics of the past filled the store. Dried apples in cans, wreaths, and candles lined the shelves. Handwoven rugs were draped over old rocking chairs.

In the book section, a title startled me: *Grandma's Tea Leaf Ironstone*. The first thing I saw on the cover of the book was a teapot, and it looked familiar.

Suddenly, I remembered that I owned a teapot similar to the one pictured. Something nudged me to buy the costly book. Uncertain of my purpose, I stood at the cash register and counted out the dollars.

Sleep did not come easily that night. I tossed and turned for hours. My eyes watched the lighted numbers on my digital clock slowly change from midnight to two o'clock. The only way to sleep was to solve the teapot mystery. I got out of bed and turned on the light. The book was on the nightstand. I stared at the picture on the book jacket. The teapot's size and shape were identical to mine. The copper leafing stood out. Surely there was a hidden meaning. I felt like my childhood detective heroine, Nancy Drew.

Something stirred in my memory. I rummaged in my billfold and found an almost-forgotten, coffee-stained business card with the name "Annise Doring Heaivilin, Author-Collector, $20.00 paid on Tea Leaf creamer and sugar 6/1/79."

Memories flooded my mind! I recalled a specific shopping adventure with my mother, where she bought a pitcher at an antique store in Riverside, Missouri. The owner of the shop, a heavy-set, gray-haired woman, told Mom she was writing a book. She asked for written permission from Mom to photograph the teapot. She gave Mom the business card receipt.

Could this possibly be the same book? My excitement was evident. Thumbing through the book I found Mother's name, Mrs. J. B. McClure, in the acknowledgment page at the front of the book.

The picture on the cover was *my* teapot! Now I knew why I had to have that book. It was my special Christmas present from the past. Although Mom was gone, her love was forever intertwined with mine through the teapot we had purchased together so long ago. Over the years and through the snow, in a dusty antique shop, I had found a book that linked me with my mother and gave me peace for the holidays.

Praise be to the God and Father of
our Lord Jesus Christ, the Father of
compassion and the God of all comfort,
who comforts us in all our troubles. . . .
2 CORINTHIANS 1:3–4

GLORIES STREAM FROM HEAVEN AFAR

He's Nearer Than You Think

Let us keep Christmas
Whatever else be lost among the years,
Let us keep Christmas still a shining thing;
Whatever doubts assail us, or what fears,
Let us hold close one day, remembering
Its poignant meaning for the hearts of men.
Let us get back our childlike faith again.

GRACE NOLL CROWELL

Is the Light in Your Eyes?

Cheryl Kirking

"Come on, kids, let's go look at the pretty Christmas lights!" Our three-year-old triplets chattered excitedly as they climbed into their car seats.

"Watch your fingers!" my husband, Dave, warned as he shut the van door. This was the first of what has become an annual family tradition. On December 23, our family of five takes a drive around our little town and into the surrounding countryside to enjoy the festive holiday lights, while carols play on the van radio.

"I like the twinkley ones!" Sarah Jean clapped her mittened hands in delight.

"I can't see," Blake said quietly.

"Oo . . . those are pwetty!" Bryce pointed a pudgy finger, his mittens already off.

"I can't see!" Blake repeated, louder this time. "I can't see!"

I turned to him, "Honey, why can't you see?"

"I can't see! The dark is in my eyes!"

I really didn't quite understand why "the dark was in his eyes," but I moved to the backseat to be beside Blake. I pointed to each light display as we drove along, oohing and aahing with him.

I gave his irresistibly soft cheek a little smooch. "Are you having fun, Blakey?"

"Uh-huh," he answered matter-of-factly. "I can see the lights now, not just the dark."

I pondered his simple words. *I can see the lights now, not just the dark.* I thought of how often I tend to focus on the dark, negative side of circumstances, instead of seeking the light, positive side. Of course, I'm an adult, not a tired three-year-old. I know that I can choose to improve my outlook. Yet, when you're tired, it sure helps to have someone beside you, someone who can see the light of the situation with greater clarity.

It took so little to change my little boy's experience of that night. I didn't have to fully understand *why* "the dark was in his eyes." But I could sit beside him and lovingly point to the beautiful lights shining in the dark world. Maybe someday, he, too, will help a young child see the light.

And we have the word of the prophets made more certain, and you will do well to pay attention to it, as to a light shining in a dark place, until the day dawns and the morning star rises in your hearts.

2 Peter 1:19

ALL THAT GLITTERS ISN'T JOY

Lynn D. Morrissey

IT WAS CHRISTMAS TIME. We had just moved into a sprawling ranch house after living twenty-four years in a charming little bungalow. I felt as if I'd left my heart and a lifetime of precious memories behind. *Oh, God, how can I experience Christmas joy in this "foreign" place?* I wondered.

As I often did when depressed, I asked God to comfort me through the Psalms. That day I happened to turn to Psalm 81: "You shall have no foreign god among you; you shall not bow down to an alien god. I am the LORD your God. . . . Open wide your mouth and I will fill it." I saw little inspiration in these words about "foreign gods" and "opening wide your mouth" to let God fill it. *Lord,* I thought, *I want joy, and you talk about idols and wide mouths! I don't understand what you're saying, but I open my heart, and ask you to fill me with your presence.*

I decided to go Christmas shopping, thinking that if I bought some special decorations for the new house to make it really *mine*, I'd experience a little joy.

I had my heart set on hand-blown golden ornaments, but was unprepared for the price. *Ouch!* Our boring old ornaments would simply have to do. *Surely we can update our pitiful nativity set,* I consoled myself. I spied a tasteful, gorgeous set made from cream-colored china, accented with gold. The baby Jesus was especially exquisite. But the price tag was not. I grew more disenchanted by the minute.

Forgetting decorations altogether, I went to the jewelry department. I had always wanted a sapphire ring. Though I knew I couldn't afford one, I thought "just looking" would be fun. Yet window-shopping only fueled my discontent.

With my "shop-for-joy" trip a dismal failure, I headed for the exit as tinny mall music whined Santa songs over blaring loudspeakers. Racing out the door, I almost ran over a little high school choir caroling in the frosty air. There was poignancy in their presence, simplicity in their singing. I, and a young mother holding a beautiful baby boy, were the only shoppers who stopped to hear the plaintive solo of a young teen singing, "Sweet little Jesus boy, we din' know who you wuz." His velvety voice floated on the air like softly falling snow. The baby cooed in response. I listened to the entire song, grateful for his gift of joy, the first I'd experienced all day.

Approaching my car, I stopped to gaze at a distant row of pear trees, their bright gold leaves flashing like amulets against a jewel-blue sky. I could hear the sharp intake of my own breath, surprised as I was by the sudden beauty.

One glance at my watch interrupted my reverie; I needed to reach the hardware store before it closed. Completely exasperated when the salesman told me he'd sold the last set of "icicle lights" (which I'd wanted to buy for *several* years), I drove home in a foul mood, without Christmas lights, without Christmas joy.

As I parked and emerged from the car, I glanced upward, mesmerized by thousands of glittering stars in the moonlit sky. *It doesn't matter if we don't have lights,* I realized. *Lord, we have your glorious galaxies!*

The truth dawned forcefully. Because I had opened my heart, God removed my fake idols and filled my day with his *real* treasures. Instead of golden ornaments and a sapphire ring, he gave me gold leaves and a turquoise sky; instead of mall music, the genuine Christmas message in a meaningful spiritual; instead of a lifeless china Jesus, a beautiful living baby—a real reminder of the vulnerable child, Jesus, born just for me; and instead of a string of light bulbs that would soon dim, a starry host that would blaze eternally.

You shall have no foreign god among
you; you shall not bow down to an alien
god. I am the LORD your God. . . .
Open wide your mouth and I will fill it.
PSALM 81:9–10

THE REMINDER

Marjorie K. Evans

IT WAS ALMOST CHRISTMAS, the joyous season of celebrating the birth of Jesus Christ. But I did not feel joyous. In fact, I felt as lonely and as somber as the dreary gray December day on which my husband and I decided to complete our Christmas shopping.

Walking from the parking lot toward the mall, tears welled up in my eyes. Christmas wouldn't be the same with Charles, Diane, and the baby—our only grandchild—thousands of miles across the ocean from us.

It was back in June when our daughter-in-law's family joined ours at the Los Angeles International Airport to bid farewell to our son. The Air Force was sending Charles to Taiwan. My heart ached for him and for Diane as they clung to each other, anguish on their faces. Not only was it difficult for them to part, but leaving Diane with one-month-old Cody made it even harder for both of them.

A few months later, after Charles had found a suitable place for his family to live, our families again met at the airport. As we said good-bye to Diane and baby Cody,

78

Diane's mother and I could almost read each other's thoughts. *Diane is so young, only 19. How can we bear to let her travel thousands of miles away with a tiny baby?*

Long letters and cassette tapes to and from Taiwan did help alleviate the concern I had for Charles, Diane, and the baby. But I knew how terribly homesick they were, and I longed to see them and to hold and cuddle baby Cody again.

But now, shopping completed, we trudged back to the car. As my husband put packages into the trunk, I stood there disconsolate, my head bowed down. Then I noticed something on the blacktop and bent over to look at it. It was a delicate butterfly pin made of tiny strips of blue and tan bamboo. Picking it up, I exclaimed in surprise, "Ed, look! Here's a butterfly pin for my collection." (Butterflies are special to me, for they symbolize new life in Christ.) Then turning it over, I read, "Made in Taiwan."

Again, tears welled up in my eyes, but this time they were tears of joy. And I breathed, "Thank you, dear heavenly Father, for giving me this reminder of your love and your care. Not only are you watching over Charles, Diane, and Cody in Taiwan, but you are thinking about me all the time."

How precious to me are your
thoughts, O God!
 How vast is the sum of them!
 Were I to count them,
  they would outnumber the grains of
sand.

PSALM 139:17–18

FLAME OF LOVE

Charlotte Adelsperger

MY CHILDHOOD CHRISTMASES were filled with simple but delightful surprises. I'll never forget the Christmas Eve when I first saw a candle in the birdbath in our backyard! A magical flame flickered from a large red candle covered with a hurricane lantern. My twin sister, Alberta, my little brother, Wally, and I pressed our noses to the frosted window in awe.

Joining in the excitement, our parents quickly explained, "Santa has marked our house. That candle must mean he's coming back tonight when everyone's asleep." We children flew straight to our beds!

Of course, we woke up early on Christmas morning and scampered into the living room. There we saw a fully decorated and lighted tree surrounded by piles of presents. The scent of fresh pine filled the room.

"Look at the tree—and toys!" Alberta said as Wally inched closer. For a glorious moment I just stared at the wonderful sight, my heart pounding. The air around me seemed to crackle with excitement.

Later on Christmas Day, our father gently took each of us to the kitchen window. "See, the candle's still burning out there," he proclaimed. A wave of joy rippled through me, and I felt our home was "marked" in a special way. I felt very loved.

A few years later we learned that our father, so creative and loving, had slipped outside and placed the candle while Mother kept us distracted. For us, it came to symbolize more than Santa. It represented our family's closeness and a sense of Christ's light in the world, and each year, the candle continued to appear on December 24. Even as teenagers, we three kids would stare into the darkness to watch a flickering flame inside a lantern standing tall in the birdbath.

Today, over fifty years since our parents, Mary and Walter Rist, first surprised us, the tradition lives on. Wally has carried it to his children.

Alberta and her husband have also made sure that our childhood home has a lighted candle in the birdbath. One year, when Mother was ninety and a widow, she sat in her wheelchair and gazed toward that light with dim and misty eyes. Later she said, "I saw it out there, but I could feel it in my heart."

Meanwhile, in another city, our own grown children and their families gather at our house Christmas Eve after church. While carols play on the radio, we rip open packages with joy and laughter. Late in the night, we bring out a shrimp supper and bow our heads for a prayer of thanks. But whenever we go to the kitchen, we can see on the deck a flickering beacon—a glowing red candle in a lantern.

After midnight when everyone is gone, my husband, Bob, and I turn off the lights except for those on the tree. In the stillness, we watch the flame burning outside. It has become a time of nostalgia and deep thanksgiving to God. Special love still marks our home.

For God, who said, "Let light shine out of darkness," made his light shine in our hearts to give us the light of the knowledge of the glory of God in the face of Christ.

2 CORINTHIANS 4:6

LET EVERY HEART
PREPARE HIM ROOM

Jessie Schut

THE CHRISTMASES I SPENT as a kid don't bear the slightest resemblance to the gift-laden feast day depicted in today's glossy magazines.

My parents were immigrants. They arrived in North America with very little except a whole lot of dreams for a better life. They brought along their customs and traditions from the old country, and that's what I remember about Christmas.

Gifts weren't part of the Dutch Christmas tradition. Instead, gifts were given on Saint Nicholas Day, December 6, when my sister and I got a package from my grandparents in Holland. In it would be our annual Christmas book (in Dutch, of course). Plus, we each got our own initial made out of chocolate. My parents also gave us simple gifts, often homemade.

Christmas was like a Sunday, which we celebrated as a day of rest. That didn't include spending hours in the kitchen slaving over a stove. I remember, instead, a table set with Mom's hand-embroidered Christmas cloth, and a candle and pine-bough centerpiece. On the menu would be special raisin breads and soft white buns, rusks (toasted bread) with chocolate sprinkles, an extra helping of cheese and cold cuts, and a hard-boiled egg for each of us. Christmas candy and oranges rounded out the meal. As a child, the glow of the candles late on a dusky winter afternoon made that meal seem like a feast.

There weren't any relatives who came to visit then. We were a nuclear family, my mom and dad and sister and I. And Christmas was a special day, which started with a church service. After church, Dad and Mom took the time to read books and play games with us all day long. Often, we visited friends who shared our traditions. The kids would always gather in the kitchen while the adults talked and drank tea in the living room. Usually the day ended with a carol sing, a mixed program of Dutch and English carols sung a cappella.

Christmas didn't resemble the magazine pictures, but it was a wonderful day, anyway. However, as I got older, I began to resent our parents' Christmas traditions. I didn't think it was fun to open our gifts December 6, weeks before my friends did. I longed for the Christmas dinners I saw depicted in books and newspapers.

I remember the flush of humiliation and embarrassment I felt when my parents said that they were inviting some long-term residents from the local hospital for the mentally ill to share "Christmas dinner" with us. Surely they would come expecting turkey and stuffing and gravy; instead, there'd be just bread and buns and hard-boiled eggs.

The three ladies arrived on Christmas Day, dressed to the nines and carefully made-up. Intelligent and sociable, their families and society had rejected them because of the stigma attached to mental illness. They only lived at the hospital because they had nowhere else to go. They sipped their tea and ate the Christmas baking, chirped excitedly about how nice it was to get away for a while, and opened the small gifts that we'd gotten for them. The moment of truth came when they gathered around the table. I waited for their disappointment to show.

One of the ladies, Barbara, dissolved into tears, and I wanted to crawl under the table where nobody could blame me for this fiasco. My mom patted Barbara on the arm and offered her a hanky.

"I'm sorry," Barbara explained when she had regained her composure, "but sitting around a table in a home with your family, I remembered what it used to be like. Thank you so much for inviting us so we could have Christmas with a family." And the other two ladies echoed her feelings.

My parents took along more than traditions from the Old World, after all. They took along the real meaning of Christmas, and that's what I remember when I dig back into my memories. The words of that old carol say it pretty well: Christmas is about joy to the world because the Lord has come.

It's about every heart preparing room, not only for Jesus, but for all of God's children.

Jesus said, "Feed my lambs."
JOHN 21:15

WISH LIST

Cheryl Herndon

MY HUSBAND AND I had been married three years. We had two children and too many bills. But we were both growing Christians and very excited about the truths of the Bible and how they applied to our daily lives.

Christmas was approaching and our finances did not look like they would support much of a celebration. There were several things I wanted to do that year. We lived in a tiny house that shared a yard with an equally small home. Our immediate neighbor was a single mother with three children. She seemed in even more dire circumstances than we were, and I really wanted to provide simple gifts for her three children. Mine were too young to comprehend whether or not they received gifts, but hers were not.

Across the street lived a mother of six who was pregnant again! I knew I could not buy gifts for all of her children, but I wanted to be able to give the expectant mother a new maternity blouse. Her stretched-out T-shirts had seen better days. She loved pretty things and kept an immaculate house but rarely did anything for herself.

My husband had a good friend, Steve, who also faced financial difficulties as a "starving" student. Steve was obsessed with his balding head. He read lots of articles on hair loss and insisted he needed a "boar's hair" brush, which would preserve his remaining crop. I thought how fun it would be to buy him his desired special brush. Lastly, I wanted to have cookies and punch for an afternoon block party a few days before Christmas.

I had been reading wonderful Scriptures about seeking first the kingdom of God and his righteousness and then all other things being provided. I read, "ask and you shall receive," and in my naive way, I did simply that. I actually went to the store and priced each of the items I wanted to purchase. The total came to $142.72. I then began praying in earnest that God would supply it—not for me, but so I could bless my neighbors and friends at Christmas.

The Sunday before Christmas, a member of our church came to me. I knew who she was but did not know her personally. I knew her because she had recently lost her husband in a tragic plane crash. She called me aside as we were leaving church and asked to speak to me alone. We ducked into the toddler's classroom, and she seemed a little sheepish. She reached into her purse and took out an envelope. She handed it to me and said she had received an unexpected check from the final settlement after her husband's death. She said all of her needs had been met and this was just some sort of interest payment that was being refunded. She went on to say that she had prayed and asked God who needed a Christmas blessing that year. He told her to give it to me!

We did not really know each other, and I had never shared my Christmas wish list with anyone, not even my husband.

I did not immediately open the envelope. In fact, I protested long and hard, because there was no logic to me that a widow should be giving me anything. She insisted she was simply being obedient and told me that was something I also should consider doing. Finally, I accepted the envelope, thanked her, and hurried off to find my husband and babies.

When we settled into the car for our ride home, I slowly opened the envelope. Inside was $143.00! Tears welled up in my eyes and my heart overflowed with gratitude to a loving God who answers prayers in such a special way.

The children in my neighborhood had their party. My neighbors' children were touched and I was able to anonymously give the pretty maternity blouse to my pregnant friend. She wore it almost every day for the rest of that pregnancy.

Now, some thirty years later, it is one of my favorite memories, because of the wonderful way God heard and answered my prayer.

So I say to you: Ask and it will be given to you; seek and you will find; knock and the door will be opened to you.

LUKE 11:9

A CHRISTMAS MIRACLE

Kathleen Boratko Ruckman

IT WAS DECEMBER 23, 1908, and a plague of diphtheria was sweeping through eastern Czechoslovakia. In the tiny village of Velky Slavkov, lying in the shadow of the High Tatra Mountains, a solitary man walked a deserted street. Pulling his hat lower on his head against the bitter wind, the man pressed ahead, passing homes with drawn shades and tightly shuttered windows.

Diphtheria, an acute, infectious disease that strikes the upper respiratory system, had ravaged the small towns along the foothills of the Tatra region. Nearly half the townspeople of Velky Slavkov had fallen to the plague, many of the victims children younger than ten.

Carrying a pail of black paint, the man climbed a flight of outdoor stairs and swabbed an "X" on the wooden doorpost of the Boratko household. Another home was quarantined. After the man left, Suzanna Boratko knelt at her doorpost, weeping and praying in Slovak. In less than a week she and her husband, Jano, were suddenly childless. Their oldest child, five-year old Mariena, had succumbed to the disease a few days earlier. In the back yard, Jano labored in the woodshed, pounding the last nail into the coffins he was building for his two sons, who had died earlier that day. Between sobs, Jano coughed and wheezed, because he too had contracted the deadly plague.

Crying in agony, Suzanna cleaned and wrapped her sons for a final time, carefully laying them into the handmade pine caskets. She and Jano lifted them onto the wagon and, with a quick slap of the reins, started the slow journey to the town cemetery.

Driving the horses through the foot-high snow, Jano and Suzanna braced themselves against a chilling wind that stung both body and soul.

"Another trip to the graveyard is more than I can bear!" Suzanna cried out, as they passed house after house marred with the black death mark. The couple empathized with those families, but they didn't have the strength to offer sympathy or encouragement. They were too wrapped up in their own grief, much like the cotton muslins tightly swathed around their sons.

Two more gravesites had been dug into the frozen earth. Now, all three children were together for eternity. Suzanna, struggling through the Lord's Prayer, hugged the cold ground and wouldn't let go. Jano finally pulled her away with what little strength he had and led her back to the wagon. She clutched her empty arms and crossed them over her broken heart. She would never hold her babies again.

Tomorrow was Christmas Eve. As Jano and Suzanna entered their barren and branded house, they needed comfort. They needed solace from their village friends. But no one dared come near. There were no Christmas greetings. No sympathies were extended. The black X spelled "DEATH" and "DO NOT ENTER." Their dark house was a frightful, forbidden tomb.

Little high-laced, brown leather shoes were still lined up against the wood stove, as they usually were when the children were tenderly tucked into the same bed. But now the large feather bed was empty, and the old stucco home never felt so cold.

"I won't see another Christmas," Jano whispered weakly to his wife. "I don't think I'll see the New Year in, either." He pushed away the soup and bread that he could not swallow. It was as though the diphtheria had tied a noose tightly around his throat, allowing neither food nor sufficient air to sustain him. The village doctor had shrugged his shoulders when he visited Jano a few days before. He had no cure.

Suzanna gathered some kindling wood and began a fire for the night, sure that her husband was about to die. But morning arrived, and Jano was still alive. Snowflakes fell from a gray sky and the wind blew a white mist over the frosted windows. Suzanna, exhausted from a restless night with little sleep, dipped her cloth again in cold water to cool Jano's fever. Then, rubbing the icy glaze off her lattice window, she fixed her eyes on the Tatra Mountains. Her mind contemplated Psalm 121:1: "I will lift up mine eyes unto the hills, from whence cometh my help" (KJV).

Suddenly her gaze was interrupted as she saw a peasant woman trudging through the snow. The old woman's red and purple plaid shawl, draped over her hunched shoulders, hardly seemed warm enough against the morning chill. She wore a babushka wrapped around her head. Her long peasant skirt was a bright display of cotton and linen patchwork. Woolen leggings and high-buttoned boots allowed her to successfully tread the snow-filled street. In one of her uncovered hands she carried a jar of clear liquid.

Suzanna stood, half-stunned, and watched the old woman as she shuffled up the forbidden walkway. She heard the knocker strike twice. She cautiously opened the door and looked into an unusual face, one wrinkled from years of farm work and severe winters. But her eyes expressed a warmth that filled Suzanna's heart.

"We have the plague in our home, and my husband is in a fever right now," Suzanna warned her.

The old woman nodded, then asked if she could step inside. She held out her little jar to Suzanna. "Take a clean, white linen and wrap it around your finger," she instructed. "Dip your finger into this pure kerosene oil and swab out your husband's throat, and then have him swallow a tablespoon of the oil. This should cause him to vomit the deadly mucous. Otherwise, he will surely suffocate. I will pray for you and your family."

The old woman squeezed Suzanna's hand and quickly stepped out in the frigid outdoors. Never before had Suzanna's heart been touched in this way. Here was a poor woman appearing in love on her doorstep in the midst of a plague. Her unexpected gift was a folk remedy against diphtheria.

"I'll try it," she called out to the old woman with tears in her eyes. "God bless you!"

Early Christmas morning Jano retched up the deadly phlegm. His fever was broken. Suzanna wept and praised God. A flicker of hope lightened her heart for a moment; surely God would someday bless her and Jano with more children.

There were no presents under a trimmed and tinseled tree that Christmas morning. But the jar of oil glimmering on the windowsill was a gift of life for generations to come.

Epilogue: In the days following the miraculous healing of Jano, Suzanna shared the folk remedy with her neighbors. In the 1920s, Jano emigrated to America to find work. Suzanna joined him later with their eight children. Their ship reached Ellis Island on Washington's birthday, February 22, 1926, and the family settled near the steel mills of Johnstown, Pennsylvania. The family eventually consisted of a set of triplets, two sets of twins, and two single births. Two of the triplet boys were named John and Paul after the two sons who died from diphtheria. The other triplet was named Samuel, the father of this author, Kathleen Boratko Ruckman.

God is within her, she will not fall;
God will help her at break of day.

PSALM 46:5

THE YEAR I ALMOST MISSED CHRISTMAS

Roberta L. Messner

IT WAS TWO DAYS after Christmas. I stared out my kitchen window at the soul-chilling rain and cheerless fog. Nothing had gone as I'd hoped this holiday season. My father was fast losing hope in his battle with cancer and I'd suffered several severe disappointments in my personal life. Tenants in our rental house hadn't paid rent in many months, and while we didn't have the heart to evict them, we weren't financially able to carry them much longer.

Worse yet, I had ahead of me another surgical operation, scheduled the first week of the New Year. Operations had been the ever-recurring story of my life. And for me, appointments with the surgeon's scalpel would never end. I was constantly growing tumors because of my illness, neurofibromatosis. Suddenly the thought of it all seemed too much. I was tired, tired to my very bones. *Was the constant daily struggle even worth it?* I wondered.

94

I gazed out the window again at the deserted bird feeder. Then, from somewhere in the recesses of my mind, came a line from a poem, although I couldn't instantly place its author. The line was "And no birds sing." Short and stark, those four words. No birds sang in my backyard nor in my life.

The brightness and glitter of my Christmas decorations mocked the ocean of gloom surrounding me. I'd lost the very hope and joy of Christmas and of living. I plunged into eradicating every trace of Christmas, then kept on cleaning house in a frenzy of busyness. By six o'clock that evening, my whole body ached from utter fatigue. Still, I found no peace.

As I crumpled into a chair, I remembered I'd promised Miss Wilson, the dear neighbor who'd been such an important part of my growing-up years, that we would drive to see the Christmas lights tonight. I hadn't visited her the entire holiday season and I couldn't let her down. At eighty-one, she lived alone and hardly got out of the house anymore, except to go to the doctor.

With packages in hand, I tapped on her front door, just as I'd done hundreds of times before. During my girlhood, her house had seemed a magical kingdom. A tinge of expectancy swept over me, as if something wonderful were about to happen.

Once inside her living room, I sank down into the tapestry sofa and handed Miss Wilson a trio of presents. She smiled warmly at me, yet her coiffed silver hair and pastel lambswool sweater failed to mask her own ailments—shortness of breath and painful arthritis. She handed a shimmering gold foil package to me. "This is a little late for Christmas," she apologized, avoiding my eyes. "I got it from a mail order catalog."

I tore open the wrapping. "It's a book on crafting holiday wreaths!" I exclaimed. "Let's make some of these next Christmas—like the old times."

"I don't expect to be here next Christmas," she answered softly, as her slippered feet smoothed and ruffled the nap of the rose plush carpet.

Her words stopped me cold. Christmas without Miss Wilson? "Of course you will," I insisted. I drew in a shaky breath and forced a smile. "And we'll both feel better when we see those Christmas lights," I said, changing the subject.

I flipped on the porch light, then took her arm and guided her down the steps and into the front seat of my car. "They say the lights in Stamford Park are fabulous this year. Why, cars were lined up for twenty minutes the other night," I jabbered. "And 'Winter Wonderland' over in Kentucky . . . you've never seen such a festival of lights."

"Honey, let's stick close to home tonight," she urged.

Over and over I silently pleaded, "Lord, if it's not too late, help us somehow find Christmas tonight." Then, on impulse, I found myself heading toward the little town of Barboursville, West Virginia, a good forty minutes away. Miss Wilson, I suddenly recalled, had taught art at the junior high school there for thirty-one years. In my work as an editor and photo stylist for home decorating magazines, I'd visited several of her former students' homes.

Once in old, familiar territory, she began to take in the splendor of Christmas. "This is Jenny Black's home," I said, pointing to the two-story white house on Main Street. "Remember, she used to be Jenny Call. You taught her in seventh grade!"

She rolled down her car window. "Just look at that picket fence draped with evergreens. And there's a candle and wreath in every window! Why, it's a perfect balance of color, texture, and scale," she said, slipping into the artist's vernacular. "Look at that lamp in the window. I can almost smell bread baking. I always told those girls, 'Now someday you're going to be homemakers.' Do you suppose she learned any of that from me?"

We drove past Barboursville Junior High, then by homes of other former students whose dazzling doors, lawns, and lampposts showcased the influence of a beloved art teacher. Pointing to an old wooden wheelbarrow bedecked with greenery and a huge red bow, she cried, "Now that's art! Using small things in a great way. Putting the uncommon touch on the common task."

"Speaking of art, do you remember that foggy day when I tried to paint a picture of that house way up on the hill?" I quizzed.

"Oh, yes," she answered with a chuckle. "You painted it a vibrant red and made it so large that it looked like it was just across the street."

"You told me, 'Now remember, things look smaller and lighter far away. We call that perspective,'" I teased.

Perspective, I thought. *That's exactly what I need.* Something to make *my* problems look smaller and lighter.

We drove on to Stamford Park, where the streets were lined with welcoming luminaries. A giant Christmas card and a life-sized manger scene retold the Christmas story in vivid detail. "Candles in paper bags," she gasped. "Well, I've never seen the like. But there's art in everything if you make the best of what you have."

As we drove along, we reminisced about the countless art lessons she'd given me over the years. It seemed we'd tried it all—tole painting, stenciling, needlework, papier-maché. And all year long we'd crafted one-of-a-kind Christmas presents. We'd always had a great time with a little bit of nothing, since Miss Wilson saved everything, and stored it all in that wonderful spare bedroom upstairs.

Once, when decorating a dollhouse, I'd grumbled that I had no money for store-bought furnishings. "Why, what you need is all around you," she had answered incredulously. So I'd studied top-of-the-line catalogs and invented new uses for old objects. Soon I'd transformed a braided place mat into an area rug, a crocheted doily into a banquet tablecloth, and cameo earrings into charming silhouette pictures. Miss Wilson was simply delighted. "See, I told you," she chided. "Everyone has creativity in them. They just need someone to bring it out."

Our final stop was a tour of "Winter Wonderland" in Ashland, Kentucky, complete with an animated carousel, skaters, snowmen, soldiers, angels, and a choir. The sounds of "Hark, the Herald Angels Sing" flooded the car. I pointed to two homes in the distance. "We just photographed them for next year's

Christmas stories," I said. "I can't wait 'til you see the pictures in the magazine."

"I always knew you'd do something special," she answered. "You were so full of ideas and ingenuity. And never mind that you couldn't draw. You always had that artist's flair."

I could hardly believe three hours had passed. "Need any bread or milk from the grocery before we head home?" I asked.

"No, but how about running by the corner drug store to check their after-Christmas mark-downs?" she suggested with a new-found sparkle in her voice. "I noticed their sale advertised in today's paper."

"What did you have in mind?" I asked as I mentally rearranged my plans.

"Oh," she paused before continuing. "Just some gift wrap and cards. You know . . . buy enough for next Christmas. I'll pay you back when we get home. It's good to plan ahead."

Once inside the pharmacy, I grabbed an armload of half-priced wrapping paper for each of us. Suddenly, I caught myself humming "Hark, the Herald Angels Sing."

"Already in the spirit of Christmas for next year?" the clerk queried.

"Well, I almost missed Christmas this year," I admitted, "but I found it just in time. I want to get an early start on next year."

As I walked back to the car, I paused to reflect on that long-ago first Christmas. What had seemed then like a lowly manger of hay was actually the bed for the King of Kings. It was all in how one looked at things.

And in only three short hours, my own eyes were opened to ever-new possibilities. Like Miss Wilson once told me, "What you need is all around you."

If you seek him, he will be found by you.

1 CHRONICLES 28:9

HEAV'NLY HOSTS
SING ALLELUIA

Angels among Us

*Blessed is the season which engages
the whole world in a conspiracy of love.*

HAMILTON WRIGHT MABIE

LITTLE RED WAGON

Patricia Lorenz

To be perfectly honest, the first month was blissful. Jeanne, Julia, Michael—ages six, four, and three—and I had moved from Missouri to my hometown in northern Illinois the very day of my divorce. I was just happy to find a place where there was no fighting or abuse.

But after the first month, I started missing my old friends and neighbors. I missed our lovely, modern, ranch-style brick home in the suburbs of St. Louis, especially after we'd settled into the 98-year-old white wood-frame house we'd rented, which was all my "post-divorce" income could afford.

In St. Louis we'd had all the comforts: a washer, dryer, dishwasher, TV, and car. Now we had none of these. It seemed to me that we'd gone from middle-class comfort to poverty-level panic.

The bedrooms upstairs in our ancient house weren't heated, but somehow the children didn't seem to notice. The linoleum floors, cold on their little feet, simply encouraged them to dress faster in the mornings and to hop into bed more quickly in the evenings.

I complained about the cold as the December wind whistled under every window and door in that old frame house. But the children giggled about "the funny air places" and simply snuggled under the heavy quilts Aunt Bernadine brought over the day we moved in.

I was frantic without a TV. "What will we do in the evenings without our favorite shows?" I asked. I felt cheated that the children would miss out on all the Christmas specials. But my three little children were more optimistic and much more creative than I. They pulled out their games and begged me to play Candyland and Old Maid with them.

We cuddled together on the tattered gray sofa the landlord provided and read picture book after picture book from the public library. At their insistence we played records, sang songs, popped popcorn, created magnificent Tinkertoy towers, and played hide-and-go-seek in our rambling old house. The children taught me how to have fun without a TV.

One shivering December day just a week before Christmas, after walking the two miles home from my temporary part-time job at a catalog store, I remembered that the week's laundry had to be done that evening. I was dead tired from lifting and sorting other people's Christmas presents and somewhat bitter, knowing that I could barely afford any gifts for my own children.

As soon as I picked up the children from the baby-sitter's, I piled four large laundry baskets full of dirty clothes into their little red wagon, and the four of us headed toward the Laundromat three blocks away.

Inside, we had to wait for washing machines and then for people to vacate the folding tables. The sorting, washing, drying, and folding took longer than usual.

Jeanne asked, "Did you bring any raisins or crackers, Mommy?"

"No. We'll have supper as soon as we get home," I snapped.

Michael's nose was pressed against the steamy glass window. "Look, Mommy! It's snowing! Big flakes!"

Julia added, "The street's all wet. It's snowing in the air but not on the ground!"

Their excitement only upset me more. As if the cold wasn't bad enough, now we had snow and slush to contend with. I hadn't even unpacked the box with their boots and mittens yet.

At last the clean, folded laundry was stacked into the baskets and placed in the little red wagon. It was pitch dark outside. Six-thirty already? No wonder they were hungry! We usually ate at five.

The children and I inched our way into the cold winter evening and slipped along the slushy sidewalk. Our procession of three little people, a crabby mother, and four baskets of fresh laundry in an old red wagon moved slowly as the wind bit our faces.

We crossed the busy four-lane street at the crosswalk. When we reached the curb, the front wagon wheels slipped on the ice and tipped the wagon over on its side, spilling all the laundry into a slushy black puddle.

"Oh no!" I wailed. "Grab the baskets, Jeanne! Julia, hold the wagon! Get back up on the sidewalk, Michael!"

I slammed the dirty wet clothes back into the baskets.

"I hate this!" I screamed. Angry tears spilled out of my eyes. I hated being poor with no car and no washer or dryer. I hated the weather. I hated being the only parent who claimed responsibility for my three small children. And without a doubt, I really hated the whole blasted Christmas season.

When we reached our house I unlocked the door, threw my purse across the room, and stomped off to my bedroom for a good cry.

I sobbed loudly enough for the children to hear. Selfishly, I wanted them to know how miserable I was. Life couldn't get any worse. The laundry was still dirty, we were all hungry and tired, there was no supper started, and there was no outlook for a brighter future.

When the tears finally stopped, I sat up and stared at a wooden plaque of Jesus hanging on the wall at the foot of my bed. I'd had that plaque since I was a small child and had carried it with me to every house I'd ever lived in. It showed Jesus with his arms outstretched over the earth, obviously solving the problems of the world.

I kept looking at his face, expecting a miracle. I looked and waited and finally said aloud, "God, can't you do something to make my life better?"

I desperately wanted an angel on a cloud to come down and rescue me.

But nobody came—except Julia, who peeked in my bedroom door and told me in her tiniest four-year-old voice that she had set the table for supper.

I could hear six-year-old Jeanne in the living room sorting the laundry into two piles, "really dirty, sorta clean, really dirty, sorta clean."

Three-year-old Michael popped into my room and gave me a picture of the first snow that he had just colored.

And you know what? At that very moment I did see not one, but three angels before me: three little cherubs eternally optimistic, once again pulling me from gloom and doom into the world of "things will be better tomorrow, Mommy."

Things did indeed get better. Single parenthood was never again as frightening or as depressing as it was the night the laundry fell out of the little red wagon. But Christmas that year was magical. We surrounded ourselves with a very special kind of love, based on the joy of doing simple things together.

Praise be to the God and Father of our Lord Jesus Christ, the Father of compassion and the God of all comfort, who comforts us in all our troubles, so that we can comfort those in any trouble with the comfort we ourselves have received from God.

2 Corinthians 1:3–4

Little Red
Wagon

107

THE GIFT TWICE GIVEN

Patricia A. Perry

"HONEY, I'VE GOT IT!" I said to my little girl. "I know what we can do for Christmas presents this year!"

I was a struggling single mom. My eight-year-old daughter, Stevie, and I were in financial straits, and Christmas was only weeks away. My family didn't expect gifts from us, but we wanted so badly to give. When the idea came, we both loved it.

"We'll make believe you have a Girl Scout project to complete," I said. "We'll tell each family member that they need to write down one thing they love about each of the other family members. Then we'll rewrite everybody's comments about Grandma on a page for Grandma, all the comments about Grandpa on one for him, and so on. The page could say, 'We love you because' at the top. We can even put each page in a frame for the person, listing which family member made each comment."

"We can afford the frames?" Stevie asked.

"Yeah, we should be able to handle that. They don't have to be fancy. The words are the gift." She was thrilled with the idea, and she started gathering the statements of love immediately.

Within a week our gifts were complete. Stevie had gathered wonderful quotes from every member of the family, things they might not have bothered to tell one another but were happy to share with this bright-eyed sprite. I made an attempt at calligraphy that was short on style—but long on good intentions!

Christmas morning came. As each of the framed pages was opened, the family member would smile in realization of the part he or she had played in the gifts Stevie and I had given. Then the recipient would eagerly read what nice things had been said about him or her.

But my sister, Noreen, had a different reaction. She cried.

Noreen had lived a whole lifetime of physical pain due to a rare blood disorder that was systematically invading every part of her body. She had risen above her physical limitations again and again to try to live a normal life. But as the years and her health fell away, she had watched friends become distant, college become an impossibility, career and marriage become mere dreams. She tried to be an optimist. But some days she confessed to feeling unloved, even by God.

So when she read the words, "We love you because," she cried. There were many words that followed, words about her compassion for others, her talent and generosity, her perseverance and hope. Her page was full of our love and admiration for her. I don't think any of us had thought, before that moment, just how much she needed to know these things.

So our Christmas gift to her was a blessing from God.

Noreen didn't make it to our Christmas celebration the following year. She died just fifteen days before Christmas. Despite her lifelong illness, her death was sudden. Unexpected. So we all faced Christmas with the painful wish that we could have told her how very much we loved her.

At the funeral service, a small table was adorned with photographs taken throughout Noreen's life: chubby-faced toddler; pony-tailed school girl; bright young woman. But there, among the frames, stood another memento, made exactly one year before. She had kept it near her bed so she would see it daily.

We love you because . . . Now the words sang out from that frame and gave us peace. We had told Noreen how much we loved her. And by embracing our love every day, she had shown us that she knew.

So her Christmas gift to us was a blessing from God, too.

Dear friends, let us love one another,
for love comes from God. Everyone
who loves has been born of God and
knows God.

1 JOHN 4:7

ANGELS OF FORGIVENESS

Susan M. Warren

I FELT AS IF I had been slapped. I gasped in horror as I stared at the empty storage room and tried to comprehend my mother-in-law's words: "We even made two hundred dollars!" She had sold all my worldly possessions, without my permission. She was trying to be kind, but in doing so, she had plowed a cavernous furrow through the garden of our friendship. I knew it would never bloom again.

Our family had just returned home after serving as missionaries for four years in Russia. We still had not found a place to live, and my mother-in-law wanted to help by clearing out room for us in her unfinished basement—in the space our forty boxes of lifetime treasures once occupied. Everything from hand-knit sweaters to homemade quilts was gone. All that was left was a forlorn crate of John Denver records and a bag of used mittens.

She handed me the proceeds of the sale and it felt like tainted money. I had waited four years to unwrap

111

my wedding china, greet my books and knickknacks, and slip back into my fine dresses. In a brutal instant, my home had gone up in flames. It was humbling to realize that I had put so much value on possessions, but I had, and now I was stripped.

Then I discovered thirty years of heirloom Christmas ornaments had been sold in the sale. Every year since childhood my mother had given me a special gift at Christmas, a new and unique tree decoration that symbolized my life for that year, as well as her love for me. The box of ornaments I had so carefully packed had been sold for a dollar; my memories, traded for the price of two cheeseburgers.

A ball of anger swelled in my heart. As I curled in my bed, sobbing out my grief, the ball began to roll. Like a snowball, it gained momentum and became an avalanche burying any tendril of love I had left for the mother of my husband.

Christmas loomed close and everywhere I went I saw beautiful, glittering Christmas trees. My tree was naked, its green arms bare against the white lights. Where was the golden star with my name etched on it, or my tiny porcelain piano? Memories assaulted me until I surrendered to fury and was entombed in cold bitterness. How could she have done this?

Sometime in January I realized I had missed the joy that came with the Advent season. Joy couldn't penetrate my icy heart. I could barely look at my mother-in-law, despite the fact she begged my forgiveness.

"I didn't know how much this would hurt you," she sobbed. "I was just trying to help."

I turned a frigid heart to her wrenching plea. Frost laced the edges of our conversations and although I said the words, "I forgive you," my soul was an iceberg and I knew I had not.

In the past, my mother-in-law had been my greatest supporter, encouraging me, helping me pack, babysitting, and stuffing thousands of newsletters. She had cried with me, prayed for me, and tolerated me living in her home. I missed her and knew that if I wanted warmth to reenter my heart, I had to forgive her. But nothing could ease the ache of losing my memories. I avoided her and resolved to live with the pain.

When we moved away in February, I slammed the door on our relationship.

The following December, three days before Christmas, a parcel with my name on it arrived at our front door. Mystified, I opened it. Then, surrounded by the music of my family's astonished gasps, I unwrapped, one by one, a collection of angel ornaments. From bears with wings and halos to gilded crystal angels holding trumpets, I hung a choir of heavenly hosts on my tree. Finally, I sank into the sofa as my children examined the decorations, oohing and aahing.

"Who's it from?" my husband asked. I retrieved the box, dug through the tissue, and unearthed a small card. *Merry Christmas—Love, Mom* was scrawled out in my mother-in-law's script. Tears burned my eyes, and as I let them free, my icy tomb of anger began to melt. My mother-in-law was not able to retrieve the past she had so carelessly discarded, but she was hoping to build a future, our future. And it would start with these angels, proclaiming the love and forgiveness that entered our world.

Easter arrived and with it, spring finally flowered in my heart. We descended upon the in-laws for a visit and I wrapped my husband's mother in a teary embrace. I had lost the little stuffed bunnies my grandmother had knit for me, but I had gained something precious—the abundant fragrance of forgiveness permeating my relationship with my mother-in-law, and the everlasting hope that love can warm the coldest heart.

> *Bear with each other and forgive whatever grievances you may have against one another. Forgive as the Lord forgave you.*
>
> COLOSSIANS 3:13

An Unlikely Angel

David Michael Smith

HE STAGGERED IN fifteen minutes after the traditional
holiday hymn sing had begun, plopping with a thud
in the wooden pew directly behind me. It was Christmas Eve at historic St. Paul's Episcopal Church in
the small, quaint town of Georgetown, Delaware, and
midnight mass was to begin in about twenty minutes.
Dozens of candles cast a warm glow throughout the
church. The organist was playing a seasonal tune, the
congregation joining the choir in a unified voice of
celebration and joy.

I could smell the strong odor of alcohol right behind
me. Trying to appear inconspicuous, I turned at an
angle while still pretending to sing so I could glance at
the source of the whiskey smell. A young man, about
twenty-five, sat alone in the pew, a drunken smile
plastered across his unshaven face. His hair was bushy
and uncombed, his clothing unbefitting of a holy
and reverent church service. I did not recognize the
fellow and later would learn that nobody else knew

who the man was either. And Georgetown is the type of friendly place where everyone seems to know just about everybody else and their family tree.

It was obvious that the man was confused. Not just with the Christmas Eve service, which for a first-time visitor can be somewhat perplexing, despite the bulletin the ushers hand out. He was disoriented in general. He stumbled aimlessly through the hymnal and prayer book like a child leafing through coloring books at the doctor's office. He was intoxicated, and his behavior made me uncomfortable. Judging by the numerous nervous stares in the young man's direction, some subtle and some not so subtle, others shared my feeling.

Then, Bob, a good-natured parishioner, left his family at their pew and joined the fellow, shaking his hand and introducing himself with a warm smile. Bob assisted the man throughout the remainder of the hymn sing, helping him locate the proper songs and directing him regarding basic liturgical functions—when to stand, sit, and kneel. With each song, the intoxicated stranger sang zealously louder and more off-key. I found his butchering of the traditional holiday carols both disturbing and amusing at the same time.

The hymn sing-a-long ended and the service began with "O Come, All Ye Faithful," as a procession of priests in robes and acolytes bearing torches entered from the back of the church. Someone in the procession waved a canister of incense, preparing the sanctuary for worship. The service continued without incident, including prayer and Bible readings about the birth of the Savior. Good Samaritan

Bob continued to befriend the man, much to the stranger's delight. I traded smiles with the man, my heart softening.

Why was I angry that he came here tonight? I thought. *This is God's house, not mine, and all are welcome in the Lord's house.* I wondered if the young man was lonely, depressed on this holiday eve, first seeking the comfort of a bottle, drowning unknown sorrows, and later journeying by our church. Perhaps he heard the festive Christmas music outside the ancient brick walls and saw the church aglow, holly wreaths hanging from the huge oaken doors, so inviting. Perhaps something deep within his heart led him to come inside, an inner voice urging him to enter. Maybe he was simply in need of warmth—or acceptance and love. I pondered who he was and where he was from. Did he have a family? Was he married? Children? He was somebody.

Then, the priest moved to the pulpit to begin his Christmas homily. He had preached for only a few minutes when he stopped his message abruptly. I thought he had lost his place, or was pausing for oratorical effect. But I was wrong. He was looking down on the congregation, about four pews back from the front, on the left side, a concerned frown rippling across his forehead. A low, curious murmur spread throughout the people. Bill, an elderly man who faithfully attended every Sunday, had slumped over. Several members of the congregation moved to his aid, thinking he had merely passed out. The situation, however, was far more grave.

The service came to a complete halt as one parishioner sprinted to call 911. Several people laid Bill down on his back in the pew and attempted to revive him. Bill was unconscious, had stopped breathing, and his pulse was weak. Even from across the center aisle in dim lighting, I could see his flesh turning gray.

Stunned, most of us just sat or stood in our pews, paralyzed with fear and disbelief. A beloved man of our church community was dying before our very eyes, and suddenly it no longer felt like Christmas Eve. I felt helpless, lost. Then a voice spoke out.

"Why don't we all get down on our knees and pray for the old guy?" the voice bellowed from behind me. It was our visitor, his voice slurred, but strong. "Maybe God can help him."

Like a slap in the face, many of us snapped out of our panicked stupor and knelt in silent obedience to the man's suggestion. As several people continued to tend to Bill, the rest of the congregation prayed in honest, pleading whispers. I prayed harder and more sincerely than I ever had, my eyes tightly shut.

Moments later, I heard a commotion to my left and was shocked to see Bill sitting up, his eyes open, the paleness in his face rapidly disappearing. Happy sobs could be heard throughout the church, our prayers gloriously answered! Despite numerous inquiries, Bill determinedly assured us that he was fine. When the paramedics arrived, racing down the center aisle with their equipment and stretcher, he refused to go to the hospital with them, insisting on staying for the conclusion of the Christmas Eve mass. And after everything settled down, the service was in fact finished without further incident.

After the closing benediction and song, an enthusiastic "Joy to the World," I turned to shake the young man's hand, but he was gone. He apparently had left during the Eucharist as the congregation filed pew-by-pew for the bread and wine.

Later, I discovered that no one had seen the man leave. It was as if he simply vanished into thin air. No one knew his identity or anything about him. He was no one's relative, or neighbor, or co-worker. Who was the man who visited us on that Christmas Eve? A dying man was revived and prayers were answered. Prayers initiated by a stranger, an unlikely angel.

> *Keep on loving each other as brothers. Do not forget to entertain strangers, for by so doing some people have entertained angels without knowing it.*
>
> HEBREWS 13:1–2

AND A LITTLE CHILD
SHALL LEAD THEM

Beverly M. Bartlett

IT WAS JUST A FEW more days until Christmas, and
I had been downtown in my native San Francisco.
Hordes of people squeezed onto those little cement
islands in the middle of the street, impatiently waiting
for slow-moving buses and streetcars to take them
home.

Finally I mounted the steps of a crowded streetcar. Although grateful to have a ride, I did not look
forward to the long trip to my apartment, as I would
have to stand the whole way. The crunch of bodies
weighed heavily on me. Oh, how I wished for a seat!
Stop after stop came and went as people got on and
off. Little by little, the mass of humanity started to
thin out, and there seemed to be room to breathe
again.

Then I noticed something out of the corner of my
eye. A small, dark-skinned hand tugged on a woman's

sleeve and a tiny voice asked, "Would you like to have a seat?" With the guiding hand of a little angel, the boy—who couldn't have been more than five or six—quietly led the woman to a free seat. Seeing the smile and grateful look on her face, that precious boy was encouraged to find another receptive soul. As soon as another seat became available, he would quickly move through the crowd to another burdened woman. He always selected a woman—perhaps he observed they were wearing less comfortable shoes, or perhaps his mother had taught him to be a gentleman and let the woman have the seat first.

Then I felt the tug on *my* sleeve. I looked down at his cherubic face, those sweet brown eyes and warm smile. "Come with me," he said, placing his soft hand in mine as he guided me to an empty seat. I thanked him and he immediately turned to find another tired woman who needed to rest her feet. The boy seemed to relish in caring for the needs of others.

A half-hour had elapsed since I first spied that little dark hand and heard his question. But unlike the first thirty minutes in the streetcar, where exhaustion hung heavy over us, there was now a lightness and joy that permeated the air as the passengers became aware of this dear fellow. People were actually smiling and chatting. This precious emissary of love had spread the spirit of Christmas to everyone in that streetcar.

As I sat there viewing the transformation that was taking place, the thought came to me, "And a little child shall lead them." Is not *this* what we adults are looking for, the innocence, trust, love, compassion, and joy of a little child—the child in each of us that too easily evaporates through the years, replaced by weariness, distrust, and hopelessness? The experience in that streetcar changed me. It was a reminder that I too could experience and share Christmas—and bring peace to others—even if in a seemingly small way. Maybe I could be "as a little child" again.

The wolf also shall dwell with the lamb, and the leopard shall lie down with the kid; and the calf and the young lion and the fatling together; and a little child shall lead them.

ISAIAH 11:6 (KJV)

THE SNOW BUNNY

Kathleen Boratko Ruckman

SNOWFLAKES FELL LIKE GOOSE DOWN on that gentle night. My visit home had flown by too quickly. It was wonderful to see my family. As always, I stayed at my dad's house in Johnstown, Pennsylvania, where I grew up. It was the meeting place of the extended family when I came to town. And it was also the place where everyone came to say good-bye.

We talked and laughed around the kitchen table on the last night of my visit, going through three pots of coffee. (My Czechoslovakian household always had a pot of coffee hot and ready, with pastry to go with it.) But one by one, my sisters and brother had to leave. When it was time to say good-bye to my youngest sister, Diane, I told her I'd help her to the car with her two little boys.

We held each other as we walked up the steep, slippery sidewalk. Snowflakes the size of nickels waltzed through the air, and a November snow had covered the ground in a thick white blanket.

Diane tucked her boys into their car seats, their little faces still rosy from running around and playing at Grandpa's house.

The wintry weather brought back memories of my childhood. I remembered standing by the kitchen window as a little girl, watching the snow fall by the street light and hoping school would be closed the next day. Now, many years later, I stood by that same street light, feeling the snowflakes on my eyelashes as I blinked back tears. Standing face-to-face with my sister, I glanced at her little boys in the car, knowing it might be another year or two before I'd see them again. Christmas was approaching, but it would be impossible for me to make the trip back.

We made small talk, trying to put off our good-byes. As we hugged each other tightly, we both spotted a white bunny hopping toward us. He stopped and sat no more than five feet from us!

The bunny sat curiously still; it was as though he came to listen to our conversation. He sat there as we talked about when we might see each other again. We both wanted to pet him, but it all seemed too wonderful to risk scaring him away.

We visited for a few more minutes. The wind grew gusty and the snow began to swirl around us. We had braved the cold for as long as we could. It was time to say good-bye.

We hugged and cried. "Take care of yourself." "You, too!" "And write soon!" When we broke our embrace and began to walk apart, we watched the bunny hop away too, as silently and gently as he had come. He seemed almost invisible—a white bunny against the snow. It was as though he came to witness a tender moment between two sisters not really saying good-bye, but "I'll see you." And then he was gone.

A month later, Christmastime came, and I thought of Pennsylvania's white rolling hills. Living in the valley of western Oregon, I could only dream of a white Christmas. I missed the snow, especially at Christmas, but memories would have to do.

As I busily prepared my home for the holiday, the doorbell rang. The mailman handed me a package from Diane! My eyes pooled as I lifted the tissue paper inside. It was a T-shirt imprinted with a snow bunny and a greeting card that read, "Somebunny loves you!"

For several years now, Diane and I have exchanged snow bunnies. It's never a question of what to get each other for gifts. Greeting cards, knickknacks, stuffed white bunnies. Exchanging bunnies has made being far away from each other more meaningful—and really, more fun.

We still wonder, though: Was a neighbor's pet bunny on the loose that night, or was this nature's gift to us? Either way, it was God's way of making a memory for two sisters who love each other very much.

My purpose is that they may be encouraged in heart and united in love.

Colossians 2:2

A Davy Crockett Hat
for David

Marjorie K. Evans

"Mom-eee, I hurt! Mom-eee, hold me! Mom-e-e-e!!"
Those were the cries I heard for days and nights.
And my heart ached for my two little boys as I held
their hot feverish bodies on my lap and prayed the
medicine would soon help them recover from the
Asian flu.

Now they were recovering. Still congested, they
breathed noisily as they napped in their bed across
the room.

But then *I* got the flu. My body was drained of
strength. I ached all over and tossed restlessly on my
bed one gray, dreary December afternoon.

The flu was the least of my problems. There was
no money to buy medicine for me, food for the three
of us, or anything for the children for Christmas.
Almost in despair I breathed, "Lord, help me. I don't
know what to do."

My husband had left us. So we moved across several states to be near my sister, who would help take care of my boys. But the long move and days of looking for a job had depleted my resources. Also, I was the sole support of my two sons—David, five, and Charles, an energetic two-and-a-half-year-old.

The secretarial job I found barely provided enough money to support the boys and me. I had already missed several days of work and did not yet have sick leave. There was no one to help, because my sister's family was also struggling to make ends meet and could not help us financially.

I had faith in God and knew he had promised to "supply all your need according to his riches in glory by Christ Jesus" (Phil. 4:19 KJV).

But as my body became increasingly weaker, so did my faith. I struggled, "Oh, how, Lord? How can you supply when there's no money coming in?"

As I lay there, tears rolled down my feverish cheeks onto the crumpled pillow, and I thought, *There's no way I can buy medicine. But I have to have it.* Finally, I called the drugstore.

The druggist listened while I explained my problem. Then he said, "Don't you know that every cloud has a silver lining? You're ill now and looking at the ugly black underneath side of the cloud. One of these days you'll be well again. Then you'll see the silver lining.

"Of course you can charge the medicine. And you can pay me whenever you're able. Have the doctor call in the prescription, and I'll send the medicine right over."

After thanking the druggist, I called the doctor. Then I sank onto the faded green couch in our small, drab living room and prayed, "Thank you, Lord."

Soon the medicine arrived, and the powerful antibiotic did help. A week later, although still shaky, I returned to work.

That day at lunch, my secretary friends spoke eagerly of Christmas plans and of gifts they had bought for their families. As they talked and laughed, I felt distressed about my inability to buy even one gift for the boys. The thought of the disappointment in their little faces on Christmas Day made tears well up in my eyes.

Then one of the women turned to me and asked, "What are you giving your children for Christmas, Marjorie?"

By now the tears were streaming down my face. Too choked up to answer, I fled to the women's lounge. There I cried and cried until my good friend, Mary, came in. She questioned me until I poured out my troubles. Mary assured me everything would work out fine, but I couldn't see how.

The week before Christmas I was more worried and distraught than ever. I wondered what we would do for food when the little we had was gone.

Preparing our meager supper of tomato soup, crackers, peanut butter, and celery, I watched the children. Their little blonde heads bobbed up and down as they made their three-wheeled truck go *buh-room, bump. Buh-room, bump,* across the brown linoleum floor.

Suddenly David stopped, looked eagerly up at me and said, "Please, Mommy, remember for Christmas

I want a Davy Crockett hat with a tail, and I want a new truck, and I want some blue socks."

I looked down at the children and wondered how to explain there would be no gifts. But before I could say anything, the doorbell rang. I opened the door to find Tom, an engineer from work, holding a big Christmas tree. Mary stood beside him, loaded down with packages.

What could I say? Overwhelmed, I just stood there. I felt like laughing and crying—and did both. Finally Tom, his tender heart masked by a gruff manner, demanded, "Well, aren't you going to ask us to come in?"

The boys jumped up and down in excitement as Mary gave each one a candy cane and a gift. She explained that the rest of the presents were for Christmas.

Eagerly the children tore off the wrapping. David squealed with delight, "Mommy! Look! A real Davy Crockett hat with a tail!" Putting on his hat, he began singing about Davy Crockett as he proudly marched around the room.

Charles, his Crockett hat askew, chimed in, "Me Davy Kwockett, too, Mommy," and happily followed David.

Then Tom and Mary brought in a frozen turkey and all the trimmings for Christmas dinner, plus bags of staple items. And they helped us decorate the tree.

When I thanked them, Tom said, "Don't thank us. A lot of us have gotten a real kick out of getting these things. We'll all have a happier Christmas because of you and your boys."

Late that evening, as I sat on the old couch in our now festive and pine-scented living room, I talked to God. I asked his forgiveness, and I thanked him that our needs had been met—right down to the Davy Crockett hats.

Be careful for nothing; but in every thing by prayer and supplication with thanksgiving let your requests be made known unto God. And the peace of God, which passeth all understanding, shall keep your hearts and minds through Christ Jesus.

PHILIPPIANS 4:6–7 (KJV)

REAL CLASS

Cheryl Kirking

MY HUSBAND RAN into the department store to buy some batteries while I waited for him to return. Weary from Christmas shopping, I preferred to wait in the warm car. It was a blustery December evening, the sky spitting little pellets of snow.

A handsome man, fifty-ish, pushed his shopping cart to a silver Mercedes parked several cars down to my right. He unloaded his purchases into the trunk, and as he walked back to return the shopping cart, I admired his attire. Everything about him was first class, from his camel-hair overcoat, to his leather driving gloves, down to his shiny loafers.

What he did next stunned me. Although he only needed to take ten more steps to return the cart all the way to the rack in front of the store, he instead gave it a careless push toward an empty parking space—the parking stall for the handicapped. The wind added to the cart's momentum, sending it crashing into the shiny black sports car parked in the next stall. Not only did this man not care if he damaged another's vehicle, he allowed his cart to prevent anyone needing the handicapped stall from parking there! He gave a backwards glance, clearly seeing what had happened, but kept right on walking to his car, got in, and sped away.

"Jerk!" I muttered to myself, thinking, *First class, all right. A first-class idiot!*

I looked up and caught the eye of the woman waiting in a car across from me, who had also witnessed this display of cloddishness. We exchanged disgusted shrugs, as if to say, "Can you believe that guy?"

Then she got out of her car and pushed the cart to the cart rack by the store front.

I smiled at her as she returned to her car, thinking to myself, *Why didn't I do that?*

We would all do well to follow her example, at Christmastime and all year through. That's *real* class.

Be ready to do whatever is good, . . .
to be peaceable and considerate, and
to show true humility toward all men.
TITUS 3:1–2

SON OF GOD, LOVE'S PURE LIGHT

Passing It On

*Somehow, not only for Christmas
But all the long year through
The joy that you give to others
Is the joy that comes back to you.*

JOHN GREENLEAF WHITTIER

CHRISTMAS MOTHER

John W. Doll

As a kid growing up in Chicago, the winter weather was cause enough to remember a few Noels with a twinge of discomfort. My brother and I, however, had other things working against us. Our dad had died, leaving our mom with only her pride and a strong back.

My brother Ned was four years older than I and went to school. It was necessary for my mom to take me with her to the only job she could find—as a cleaning lady. In those days, work was scarce and money even more so. I remember watching Mom hour after hour scrubbing floors and walls on her hands and knees, or sitting on the outside of a windowsill washing windows four stories off the ground in freezing weather—all for twenty-five cents an hour!

It was Christmas Eve of 1925 that I shall never forget. Mom had just finished working on Chicago's Near Northside and we headed home on one of the big, red, noisy, cold streetcars. Mom had earned her $2.25 for nine hours of work plus a jar of tomato jam as a Christmas present. Her fare was seven cents and mine was three cents. I remember, after she lifted me onto the rear platform of the streetcar, how she searched through her precious few coins for five pennies and a nickel. As we sat together on the cold seats we held hands; the roughness of her hands almost scratched my bare hands as she held them tightly in hers.

I knew it was Christmas Eve, and even though I was only five, the past few Christmases had conditioned me not to expect anything more than some extra food, a visit to the Marshall Field's animated window display, and other kids' excitement.

With Mom's hand in mine and the knowledge that our Christmas basket had been delivered by Big Brothers, a charitable organization, I felt a warm sense of security as we headed home.

We had just passed a major intersection where Wieboldts, a large department store, was letting out the last of its shoppers before closing for Christmas Eve. Their feelings of holiday cheer and cries of joy and happiness could be felt and heard through the steel walls and noise of the traveling streetcar. I was insensitive to the joy, but as I looked up at Mom I could feel her body racked with pain. Tears streamed down her weathered face. She squeezed my hand as she released it to wipe away her tears with those chapped and cracking hands. I will always remember her hands with the swollen knuckles, enlarged veins, and coarse surface, though now they represent her sacrifices, honesty, and love.

That night, the bitter cold struck our faces as we stepped down from the streetcar and onto the icy, snow-covered street.

I walked close to Mom to stay warm and looked into the front-room windows that framed brightly lighted Christmas trees. Mom walked straight ahead without a side glance, one of her ungloved hands holding mine, the other holding a paper shopping bag that contained her soiled white uniform and the jar of tomato jam.

Our flat was a corner unit in the middle of the block. Each Christmas, Nick, the barber, sold Christmas trees on an empty lot next to his shop. The tree lots were sold out long before Christmas Eve, leaving only broken or dead brown branches covering the ground. As we passed the quiet, emptied lot, Mom dropped my hand and picked up a bundle of broken, discarded pine-needle branches.

As we climbed the dingy wooden stairs to our flat, I'm sure my relief was only minimal compared with Mom's. Our flat had only a small pot-bellied stove in the kitchen for heat. Ned and I fed the stove with coal that dropped from railroad cars a couple of blocks away and with wooden fruit boxes that we found in the alley next to our house. It was natural for each of us to bring home anything that would burn.

We opened the door to the front room, which felt like a refrigerator. Neither the front bedroom, nor Ned's bedroom, next to the kitchen, were any warmer. The door to the kitchen was kept closed to keep what little heat there was in the bathless bathroom, the rear bedroom, and the worn, linoleum-covered kitchen. Other than two beds and a lion-clawed wood table with four chairs, there was no other furniture or floor covering in the entire flat.

Ned had started a fire and had pulled up close to the stove to absorb what little heat it afforded. He was absorbed in an old issue of *Boy's Life*. Mom unbundled me and sat me next to the stove, then prepared the table for our Christmas feast.

There were few words spoken because the season was about joy, giving, receiving, and love. With the exception of love, there was an obvious void in the remaining Christmas features. We sat facing the little wood stove as we ate canned ham, vegetables, and bread. Our faces flushed with the heat as the cold attacked our backs.

I remember that my only concerns that evening were having to go to bed early because of no heat and the shock of cold sheets.

As usual, we washed our hands and faces in cold water, brushed our teeth, and made a Rambo-like charge to our respective frozen beds. I curled up between the two sheets of ice with my socks and Ace cap still on. A cold draft of air attacked my behind because one button was missing from my thin, second-hand long underwear. There was no great anticipation about what I would or would not receive for Christmas, so I fell asleep fast and soundly.

Because the streetlight was directly opposite my bedroom window and the Oscar Mayer slaughter-houses were only half a block away, it was common for large trucks to wake me up several times a night. But at my age and with the cold, it was no challenge to escape back to my dreams.

During the twilight before dawn, I awoke. The streetlight clearly illuminated Mom's ticking tin clock (with one missing foot). I hadn't heard the milkman rattling bottles or his horses' hoofs in the alley, so I knew I could sleep at least a few hours longer.

However, when I looked over to see my mother sleeping beside me, I realized that she hadn't been to bed yet. Suddenly I was wide awake in a state of panic, wondering if Mom was sick or if she had finally had enough and left.

The trucks had passed but my panic had not, as I lay there staring at the streetlight with my wool cap over my eyebrows and flannel blankets up to my eyes. I couldn't imagine life without Mom.

I lay in the icy stillness, afraid to get up and confirm my fears, but totally incapable of going back to sleep. Then, I heard a grinding, twisting sound coming from the kitchen. It was as constant as a machine; it would stop for a few seconds, then continue, then pause again.

As best as I could tell time at that age, I figured it was about 5:00 A.M. With the darkness of winter there was no assurance of what time it really was, other than it was long past the time Mom should have been in bed.

As much as I feared the truth, I knew I had to find it. I rolled under the covers to the edge of the bed and dropped my stocking-covered feet to the cold, bare wood floor. With the streetlight illuminating the bedroom, I could see my breath as clear as if I were out in the street.

Once into the darkness of the front room, I was guided to the kitchen by a light glowing from under the door, which was ajar. The grinding, twisting sound became louder as I approached. The stove had been out for hours and I could see Mom's breath as well as my own. Her back was toward me. She had wrapped a blanket over her head and back for some small insulation against the cold.

On the floor to the right was her favorite broom, but the handle had been whittled off just above the sweeping portion. She was working at the old wood table, and I had never seen such total concentration and dedication. In front of her was what appeared to be some sort of a disfigured Christmas tree. As I stared in awe her effort became apparent: She was using her broken kitchen knife to drill holes in her broom handle, into which she had inserted the branches from Nick's empty tree lot. Suddenly it became the most beautiful Christmas tree I had ever seen in my life.

As she continued to twist and dig slots for the remaining branches, my eyes dropped to her feet, where a small can of red paint was still open. A wet brush lay next to it. On the other side of her chair, there were two towels on the floor that were almost covered with red toys: a fire engine with two wheels missing from the back; an old steel train with a number of wheels missing and the caboose's roof bent in half; a jack, out-of-the-box, with no head; and a doll's head with no body. I felt no cold, no fears, no pain, but rather the greatest flow of love I have ever felt in my life. I stood motionless and silent as tears poured from my eyes.

Mom didn't stop for a second, and I silently turned and walked slowly back to my bedroom. I shall never forget that Christmas of 1925—nor the priceless gifts my mother's love provided.

> *Out of the most severe trial,*
> *their overflowing joy and their*
> *extreme poverty welled up in rich*
> *generosity. . . . For if the willingness*
> *is there, the gift is acceptable*
> *according to what one has,*
> *not according to what he does not*
> *have.*
>
> 2 CORINTHIANS 8:2, 12

CHRISTMAS VS. A COLD HEART

Liz Hoyt

LEONARD STOOD IN MY DOORWAY on that cold December morning, glaring at me defiantly with angry brown eyes. Gazing at him, I told the caseworker very firmly that I absolutely could not take any more foster children. But by suppertime that night, Leonard and his blonde, six-year-old sister had moved in. I telephoned my husband to explain, "He is only eight years old; the other four children will help, and well, honey, it's Christmas." He just sighed and said, "I'll be home early, Wimp!"

It's true that Leonard stole my heart. But that was just the beginning. Leonard set about stealing toys, books, and money from everybody in the family, from our neighbors, and from the kids in his second-grade class. That December, I spent more time in the principal's office than I did in the kitchen.

Leonard had watched his mother die in a fire that erupted in their shack during a drunken brawl. Afterwards, his father beat him day after day, telling Leonard he was to blame. Through it all, Leonard was the sole caregiver for his little sister. Stealing food for the two of them was just one of the things he had learned to do for their survival.

I knew I could not feel the depth of Leonard's pain, and he could not know I would never give up on him, but I wanted to provide the best Christmas he could imagine. Leonard responded by sullenly watching as the family decorated the tree, made gifts for each other, and baked cookies. The friends and neighbors Leonard had stolen from and fought with pitched in with understanding hearts, and provided gifts, money, and food for our expanding family. All of our children—two birth and four foster—received equally.

We went to church, sang carols, read the Christmas story during family devotions, had pictures taken with Santa, and took part in the school parties and the annual Christmas pageant at church. Nothing touched Leonard. If he addressed me at all, it was to snarl, "Hey lady!" His rebellious expression never changed and the few words he uttered were punctuated with expletives. His anger slowly began to overpower Christmas, and I was helpless to stop the heaviness that settled over our household.

The calendar solemnly moved to December 25. Santa came and we opened presents, but our joy was hollow and forced. We wearily sat down to our Christmas dinner and I silently prayed that the day would end with no more pain. My husband was quietly carving the turkey when our ten-year-old birth daughter suddenly remembered a tiny box that had arrived from her grandmother before Christmas and she could not remember opening it.

We frantically searched the entire house but the box was not to be found and the day slid from bad to worse. The next morning, a sibling argument broke out early and, in a fit of anger, Leonard yelled at my daughter, "I took your stupid box, and it's in my desk at school! So what'cha gonna do 'bout it, crybaby? Tell your ol' lady and see if I care."

During the month of peace on earth, the principal of our large elementary school and I had reached a strained—but polite—relationship that included exchanging each other's home phone numbers. He was not pleased to go on a scavenger hunt the day after Christmas, but knowing well my fierce "foster-mother temperament" he agreed to open the school for us. As we arrived at the school, the principal's displeasure was evident. Even the red and green Christmas decorations seemed to mock us as we three trudged silently down the long hall. When we reached the classroom, Leonard stomped across the room and dumped the contents of his messy desk at my feet. He clawed through the jumble of crayons, books, papers, marbles, pencils, and miscellaneous toys and triumphantly grabbed a small, delicate box. He shoved it at me and a tiny antique cross fell to the floor.

Leonard snarled, "Now where ya gonna take me? When do I leave? And, uh, who you gonna give all them presents to that had my name on 'em? I knowed I couldn't of kept 'em. I knowed it all along."

I cupped his angry chin in my hands and said quietly, "Leonard, the presents are yours to keep whether you stay or leave. I won't force you to stay—but I want you to be one of my little boys for as long as you need me." He stared at me for a long time with those captivating brown eyes. When the sobs started, I reached out and he fell into my arms. We held each other tightly as years of pent-up pain poured out of his tortured soul. The principal stood by silently, as if guarding his flock. After a long while, Leonard wiped his face with a dirty hand, sniffed hard, and with a quivering voice said, "Can . . . can we go home now . . . Mama?"

Christmas was late that year but it arrived in glowing splendor on the cold floor of that empty schoolroom. I took Leonard home—and the angels sang.

"Lord, when did we see you hungry and feed you, or thirsty and give you something to drink? When did we see you a stranger and invite you in, or needing clothes and clothe you? When did we see you sick or in prison and go to visit you?"

The King will reply, "I tell you the truth, whatever you did for one of the least of these brothers of mine, you did for me."

MATTHEW 25:37–40

When Receiving
Is the Gift

Cheryl Kirking

WE WISH YOU *a merry Christmas and a happy New Year!* We sang our final number enthusiastically, if not in tune. Each year, members of our youth group piled into station wagons and went caroling to area homes around the rural Wisconsin countryside. Our car's final stop was to the little farm house of Martha, an older widow known for her warm heart and good Norwegian cooking.

Martha motioned us in. "Now, come in for a minute and have some cookies!" I peered past the group and spied two plates heaped with cookies on her kitchen table. Cut-out cookies, as well as Norwegian delicacies, *krumkake* and *sanbakels*.

"Oh, no, Martha. Our boots are all snowy. But thanks anyway." Paul, the leader of our group had declined. He was the designated leader because he was the only one with a driver's license.

"Oh, but I have cookies and cocoa for you all!" Martha urged.

"No, no, we don't want to trouble you. But thanks anyway!" Paul repeated. "We'd better be going." With that, he motioned for us younger kids to get back to the car. As the eight of us piled into his parent's station wagon, several of the boys complained.

"Why couldn't we have some cookies?" one asked.

"We didn't come here to eat all her cookies; we came to sing." Paul answered. "Besides, we'll have plenty of cookies back at the party." *Yeah, but they won't be as good as Martha's,* I thought to myself.

"How was the party?" my mother asked when we returned home. "We went to Martha's house," I reported, "but Paul wouldn't let us have any cookies. She had two huge plates with *sanbakels* and *krumkake* and everything!"

"She had them all ready for you?" Mama asked, sounding the tiniest bit irritated.

"Don't worry, Mama," I said quickly, feeling guilty for my selfishness. "We didn't eat any!"

"Why not?" Mama asked.

Now I was confused. "Well," I explained, "we wanted to, but Paul said no. He said we shouldn't make her go to all that trouble."

Mama sighed. "Children, Martha was obviously expecting you—she had already fixed the cookies and cocoa."

"Well, we didn't know what to do," I said.

"I know," my mother answered. "I just want you kids to understand that sometimes the nicest thing you can do for someone is *let them* be nice to you.

I'm sure Paul meant well, but it would have meant a lot to Martha to see you enjoy her cookies. Does that make sense?"

It did. And it still does today, thirty years later. Can you think of someone you might bless by receiving what they have to offer? Often, the best gift we can give is allowing someone the *privilege* of giving.

> *It is more blessed to give than to receive.*
>
> ACTS 20:35

A Holiday Tradition

Pat A. Carman

IN KEEPING WITH the annual tradition we had established at our workplace, our office searched for a family that may not have a Christmas celebration without some assistance. We contacted several agencies and churches, and at last found a family of eight who had experienced not just one year of misfortune, but several. Living in a small Oregon town in the foothills of the Cascades, the personal tragedies they had experienced in the previous two years had forced them to begin all over again financially. They expected their holidays would be sparse and pretty bleak. But what they lacked in material possessions, they made up for in their strong sense of family and love for each other.

For one month, we gathered gifts in brightly wrapped boxes and packages, and cash donations in a decorated tin. As we shopped for the mom, dad, and these six children, we had such fun deciding just what each would get. We could just envision their

Christmas morning when they would unwrap the gifts! For the boys, we bought warm winter gloves for snowy days when they walked to school, and models to put together when housebound. For the little girls, there were pretty dolls and fuzzy animal slippers. For the oldest daughter in her early teens, some perfume and a watch. Dad would receive a new ski sweater, to remind him that he needed to take time from work in his studio to have fun on the nearby slopes.

And for Mom, a much-deserved new Christmas outfit. Our gift for the whole family was a game for all to enjoy, and we also added the makings of a Christmas dinner.

The family would not know, of course, who their personal Santas had been. We made arrangements for the pastor of their small country church to deliver our presents several days before Christmas. We would ship the gifts to him, from our town 120 miles away, thus remaining anonymous.

Our excitement was building and we waited in anticipation to hear "the rest of the story," but not one of us could have guessed what really happened. We found out later that we were not the only characters involved.

On the Friday before Christmas, the mother of our family came home from work. Employed as a software engineer in a nearby town, she excitedly announced that her employer had given her a $300 Christmas bonus. Her husband welcomed the news. Now they could buy gifts for the children! Together they composed a list, making sure that the "wants" equaled the "needs." They would do some shopping next week, in the two days before the holiday. What a timely gift!

That weekend, the family attended their Sunday church service, feeling a great release from pressure. In a special prayer time they heard that one of their friends from the congregation was soon to have surgery. He was out of work and unable to pay medical bills and his family was without food. Knowing the desperation their friends must have felt, they had immediate sympathy for their situation. When they returned home, they held a "family meeting" and decided as a group to give their Christmas bonus to their friends. Food and medical bills were more important than Christmas toys.

Within a few hours after making their decision, the pastor stopped by to visit his long-time friends. Before he could explain the reason for the day's visit, they told him they would like to donate their good fortune and asked him to deliver a check for them. The pastor was amazed at their generosity and agreed to deliver the check if the family would come out to his car with him. Puzzled but agreeable, they walked to the driveway, where they found his car overflowing with Christmas presents—the presents we sent over the mountains as our expression of Christmas love.

The faithless will be fully repaid
for their ways,
and the good man rewarded for his.

PROVERBS 14:14

A HOLIDAY
TRADITION

ORANGES IN OUR SOCKS

Karin McClain

IN OCTOBER 1951, as soon as Dad finished harvesting what little wheat was left after damaging hailstorms hit our North Dakota farm, Dad and Mom loaded the family in our '41 Chevy, and we headed east. Even though Dad had hail insurance on his wheat crops, it wasn't enough income to support our family through the winter and still have money to buy seed for the following spring planting. He felt he needed to get a job with a weekly paycheck to carry us through the winter.

So Mom packed the bare necessities for our family of seven into a homemade trailer. There was Craig, the oldest, at 11; then me, age 9; Kristin, age 7; Lucretia, age 4; and Maurice, age 2.

I don't know what made Dad pick Kankakee, Illinois. We had no relatives or any connection to that area. But on the outskirts of town, there was a motel that had been bypassed by new highway construction. Since their business had been drastically reduced, they were willing to rent to us on a monthly basis. We rented a furnished unit consisting of a kitchen, living room, and two bedrooms. Dad found work at the next town over.

We kids had always looked forward to Christmas, and this year was no exception. We had a small Christmas tree sparsely decorated with the few ornaments Mom had managed to crowd into the over-packed moving trailer. We hung our stockings as we always did—not fancy ornamental stockings, but those from our underwear drawer.

At our house, Santa brought only gifts that would fit into a sock. Santa was clever, though, and he could make a small sock hold more by tightly rolling a coloring book and then letting it unroll to the full width of the leg opening. By letting the book stick up above the opening of the sock it extended the space. In addition to coloring books, Santa might leave new toothbrushes, crayons, sets of jacks, yo-yos, barrettes, small dolls, toy cars, or a bottle of colored ink for writing to pen pals. The five of us always eagerly dumped our stockings, then looked over what the others had received.

Along with these special gifts, Santa always placed an orange in the toe of each stocking. But this particular Christmas, Mom had only three oranges to fill the five stockings. Since checking out what the others got was half the fun, Santa had a real problem.

Before we went to bed on Christmas Eve, Mom explained her dilemma to Craig and me. We were the oldest and we knew about "Santa," but Kristin, Lucretia, and Maurice still believed. Santa couldn't forget the oranges for our stockings, because the younger kids would wonder why we didn't get one. But Mom, as always, found a solution. She told us that she had saved the produce tissue that had wrapped the precious oranges. She wrapped onions in those little squares of tissue, and, being forewarned, my brother and I did not take off the tissue in front of the younger siblings. Because of my mother's creative problem solving, Christmas morning proved as joyous as always.

My younger siblings didn't discover the secret of the onions until forty-seven years later, in 1998, when the story was told at the Thanksgiving table. That December, each of us got a wonderful chocolate orange from Kristin, who has since made sure that her siblings are never without an orange for Christmas.

Command them to do good, to be rich
in good deeds, and to be generous
and willing to share. In this way they
will lay up treasure for themselves
as a firm foundation for the coming
age, so that they may take hold of the
life that is truly life.

1 TIMOTHY 6:18–19

HOME FOR THE HOLIDAYS

Margolyn Woods

WE COULD HARDLY WAIT. We were going to visit Grandma and Grandpa for Christmas. It had been two long years since Dad was transferred to California, two difficult years of trying to fit into a new school and make new friends.

The car ride would take the better part of two days, but we were going *home!* Home to our old neighborhood, friends, and family. Our car was tightly packed with Christmas surprises for aunts, uncles, cousins, and friends. We laughed as we made a "spot" for each of us in the car. There was barely room to sit, let alone spread out for the long ride.

The excitement kept us all happy and talkative the whole first day.

"Heavy snow," the newsman predicted as we were getting up the following morning. The three of us jumped up and down with glee at the thought of snow forts and sledding. Mom and Dad had looks of trepidation.

"We'd better stop and put on chains," announced Dad when the storm became intense and the roads became slick. When visibility was almost gone, Dad decided it was wiser to stop for the night at a motel and begin again at first light the following day.

"Don't take much out of the car," Mom announced. "Take just enough for the night."

It was still dark when Dad woke us the next morning. He headed out to warm up the car while we got ready.

The door opened a few minutes later. The look on Dad's face told us that something was terribly wrong.

"We've been robbed," he announced. "The entire car has been emptied."

He reached out to hug Mom as she began to cry.

"How could someone do this?" sobbed Mom. "All of our Christmas gifts!"

My heart sank. How could this have happened to us? Didn't they know how long we'd planned this trip? What were they going to do with Grandma's music box or Blair's fire engine?

As more news of the weather came across the television, the decision was made. We couldn't go on. We were going to have to head back. Back to a Christmas without family, gifts, or a tree. Back to a sad reality.

It was dusk on Christmas Eve when we pulled into our driveway.

"What happened?" asked Mr. Olsen, our next-door neighbor. In tearful sobs we shared our shattered dreams and hopes for Christmas.

The house was dark and cold. Our attitude was somber as we helped Dad empty the car and put away what little we had left. Suddenly the doorbell rang.

"This little tree is looking for a home," announced Mr. Olsen, dragging a four-foot tree. Behind him came his wife and children, ladened with decorations and gifts for under the tree.

"You are so thoughtful," said Mom, tears in her eyes.

The doorbell rang again and again. Before long we had a refrigerator full of food, we were invited to Christmas dinners, and we were surrounded by loving neighbors and friends.

The smell of breakfast woke me the next morning. "Merry Christmas," said Mom and Dad, smiling, as I made my way into the living room. The fireplace was glowing and the Christmas tree lights sparkled as we gathered to marvel at God's goodness. Who would have ever thought? We had a beautiful tree, wonderful food, presents, and good friends. Most importantly, we had each other. We were home for the holidays after all.

Every good and perfect gift is from above.

JAMES 1:17

SPREADING
CHRISTMAS CHEER

John W. Doll

I NEVER GAVE my son a spending allowance, but Cary
knew that if he wanted money, he would simply have
to perform a chore.

With Thanksgiving just past, I wasn't too surprised
to have my son ask me to help him figure out a project to make some Christmas money.

Earlier, we had found an abundance of mistletoe
on some oak trees. I suggested that, with a little red
ribbon attached, it would sell for a dollar a bunch. The
mistletoe was free, I could subsidize the ribbon and
plastic bags, and Cary could sell the product door-to-
door. It was a "no-lose" program: Cary could get his
Christmas money, his customers would get a bargain,
and jointly we could help our neighborhood get into
the Christmas spirit with a lot of "kissin' and hug-
gin'." Cary and I drove out to a growing subdivision

called Thousand Oaks, and in fifteen minutes had the raw material for his total Christmas inventory.

Cary made up little bunches of the mistletoe and his mother put on little red and green ribbons. In a couple of hours, Cary had his wooden wagon loaded up. He began selling that Saturday at about 10:00 A.M. and was home in time for lunch with his pockets filled with money.

The following year, Cary didn't come to me meekly and ask for a Christmas project. The success of the prior year had made him aggressive and confident. "Dad, this year we're going to do it right; we're going to do it *big!*"

I cautiously asked, "What do you mean, *we* are?"

"No big deal," Cary answered. "You only have to give me the ribbons and plastic bags." Cary continued, his enthusiasm bubbling over, "I'm going to get my friends to make the house sales and help with the packaging, and I'm going to sell big boxes to the gas stations and grocery stores." I hated to be negative, but I cautioned him. "Cary, I don't think the gas stations or groceries will pay you in advance for your product."

He was not to be discouraged. "No problem, Dad. We'll loan it to them and we'll collect all the money after."

I bought five hundred plastic baggies and designed a header that was titled "Kiss'n' Stuff." This header would also act as a way to close the bags once the mistletoe was inserted. I thought, *Well, at least he'll need my help to collect the mistletoe.*

But on the Saturday we were to collect the greenery, Lanie, my wife, said, "The boys couldn't wait for you to wake up so they attached wagons to their bikes and have gone out hunting mistletoe on their own." I felt a slight pang of rejection.

Well, I made up my mind I would just stay out of the rest of the program. I admit that I had hoped to be needed just a little bit more.

All weekend they collected the greens from a new location that they said had an endless supply. The following weekend I was awakened by the laughing and talking that was coming from our garage. I looked out the bedroom window and into the open garage. Our Ping-Pong table had been set up in the middle of the garage, and Cary was waving his arms around and directing about ten kids who were putting the green stuff into the little plastic bags. Two little girls at the end of the production line were stapling the "Kiss'n' Stuff" headers on the open end of the bags, which were then packed into small cardboard boxes marked with the names of Tom, Jim, Joe, Mary, etc. I slipped back to bed and slept for several more hours, feeling that my old-age security was assured with a son who possessed such an entrepreneurial spirit.

It was the weekend before Christmas when the real action started. All day long the kids came in and out, picking up fresh loads of the "Kiss'n' Stuff." Cary had apparently lost the house-to-house market when his sales kids found out their boss was only going after the big volume sales.

By the end of the day, all the "Kiss'n' Stuff" had been consigned, and as the kids returned to the garage with their list of consignees, you would have thought each one had found his own personal pot of gold. They spoke of how easily each of their customers accepted the product, without payment, and how they thought it was such a cute idea—and, best of all, how well they thought it would sell. The kids talked about the grand gifts they would buy their folks and friends, and they had a few gift ideas for themselves as well.

The only thing they had yet to decide was how big a bag they would need to pick up all the money.

It was only a few days before Christmas—the big collection day. Cary didn't need a second wake-up call with the anticipation of his Christmas wealth.

As the family chatted at the breakfast table, I noticed Cary scratching. First his head, then his stomach, arms, legs, and then back again to his arms and head. By now Lanie had also noticed, asking, "Cary, did you take your bath last night?"

He just dropped his head and said, "Aw, Mom," and once again began scratching his neck and forearm. I reached across the table and rolled up his shirt sleeve. There, just above his wrist, was an inflamed area that was almost solid with tiny little water blisters.

Lanie put her hand to her cheek and said, "It looks like we're going to have chicken pox with our Christmas this year!"

I rolled up Cary's other shirt sleeve and the watery condition was apparent.

Cary said, "Hey, I thought you only get chicken pox once, and I had them last year."

Lanie and I looked at each other. "He's right," I said. "He did have them last year. Cary, take off your shirt." He slowly removed his shirt as he asked, "Dad, will you pick up all my money?"

As his shirt dropped to the floor, I noticed the little blisters were only on his wrists and forearms. It was more like a poison ivy rash . . . or . . . poison oak!

"Cary," I almost screamed, "where did you find your mistletoe?"

"In the empty lot, down by the ditch, Dad," he replied. That was too far away to confirm my fears, but I ran out the back door and lifted the garage door. I felt like I was visiting the scene of a crime. Cardboard boxes that were still loaded with the greenery, a pile of plastic baggies, and the "Kiss'n' Stuff" labels were spread out across the Ping-Pong assembly table. I walked up to the remaining bunches of what the kids thought was mistletoe. The kids, under my son's direction, had mass-marketed three or four hundred cute packages of poison oak to every gas station and small grocery store in the neighborhood! As I stood there I began imagining all the friends my son had just lost, the parents standing in line to take a punch at me, and how far I would now have to travel to buy a loaf of bread or a tank of gas.

I walked slowly back to the kitchen. Lanie had anticipated the problem and was dabbing our son's arms and the back of his hands with calamine lotion. I sat down next to Cary and put my arm around his shoulder. He looked up at me with the anticipation of some great, wise words of wisdom. I patted him on the back and with a pleading look said, "Son, have you ever seriously considered becoming a Boy Scout?"

"No, Dad, but you didn't answer my question."

"What question?" I replied.

"Dad," he asked impatiently, "will you pick up all my money?"

Except for the time I had to go to the local drug store to get more calamine lotion, I didn't get too much reaction from our "Poison Oak Christmas." Seymour, our druggist, was a friend of mine, and when I took the calamine lotion to the counter he said, "You know, Bud, this business is funny. We haven't sold any of this stuff for years, and now suddenly it's selling like aspirin!"

A cheerful heart is good medicine.
PROVERBS 17:22

WITH
THE DAWN
OF REDEEMING
GRACE

Righteousness Revealed

Christmas is continuity. It's the on-going affirmation of the greatest ideas and truth. People feel reborn, excited, whole. Christmas is victory. It is the message that we are never defeated.

NORMAN VINCENT PEALE

CHRISTMAS IS . . .

Cheryl Kirking

"WHAT IS CHRISTMAS?" I asked the little ones gathered at my feet. I had been asked to give the children's message during morning worship that Sunday in December.

The children had a variety of responses: "Christmas is a happy time." "It's Jesus' birthday!" "It's when you get presents!"

A curly-headed tot wiggled her way from the back of the group to my feet. She boldly stood and loudly announced, "*I* will tell you about Christmas!" I smiled and pulled her onto my lap, holding the microphone close to her. "Okay, Molly, tell us what you think Christmas is."

"Christmas is . . ." Molly stuck her finger in her mouth, suddenly very shy, and buried her face in my shoulder.

"Yes, Molly?" I coaxed.

"Christmas is . . ." she began hesitantly.

167

I brushed the tousled curls from her eyes. "Yes, honey?"

She pressed her lips to the microphone and whispered loudly, "Christmas is very . . . *shiny!*"

The older children giggled and the adults tried hard not to. At the sound of their laughter, Molly's round, brown eyes misted with tears, her lower lip quivering. She buried her face again in my shoulder and the tears spilled over.

Before I could respond, Molly's six-year-old brother, John, stood and made his way to me. With all the solemnity and wisdom of a sage he pronounced, "Christmas *is* very shiny. It is the love of God shining through the darkness."

A hush fell over the congregation as our jaws dropped in awe of this little wise man.

With a kiss on her moist cheek, I handed Molly over to her big brother, who led her by the hand back to their seats. There was no need to add to his sermon. Message given, message received.

> *For God, who said, "Let light shine out of darkness," made his light shine in our hearts to give us the light of the knowledge of the glory of God in the face of Christ.*

2 Corinthians 4:6

Evergreen

Jan Leong

I LOOKED AROUND and saw heaps of debris piled along the street. Like me, our neighbors had dragged Christmas to the curb. My trash can refused orders. Picking up its protesting lid, I forcibly insisted that it contain the boxes, ribbons, and bows that were the remnants of our Christmas wishes. As my son Kenton pulled the last can to the curb, I felt thankful to be done with the chaos of the holidays, and I retreated toward the door.

Barely across the sidewalk, my composure was shattered by Kenton bellowing excitedly, "Mom!" I shuddered. Kenton and trash always brought the same result: treasure or clutter depending on your perspective. I spun around to see him struggle down the street with his newest treasure, a four-foot, potted Christmas tree. His eyes gleamed, "Can I keep it?"

I set my jaw firmly as I looked him squarely in the face. I spoke slowly. I wanted him to understand that my diagnosis was my answer. "It's dead!"

"No, there's still some green," he defended.

Was he blind? Couldn't he read my expression? Maybe it would be more clear if I used a different tone of voice. My whole body sighed as my voice rose in a pleading whine, "Kenton, we just got the place cleaned up!"

He placed a protective hand on a bough of his not-so-evergreen. "I can get it to grow . . . we can use it next year . . . we'll save money. You'll be glad you said yes!" he persisted.

Fatigued from my recent participation in the Battle of Buying, weakened by crowd combat and sale skirmishes, I lost the will to fight. I gave way. "Okay," I said. "You can keep it for a while and see if you can bring it back to life."

"Thanks, Mom!" He grinned as he dragged his prize in the direction of the back yard. The tree disintegrated more on the driveway with each step he took. I rolled my eyes, shook my head, and went inside.

A week or two later I ventured into the garden for a moment of morning solitude. Southern California's golden sunshine warmed my face. Crisp, clean air filled my lungs. "Hey, Mom! Doesn't the tree look great?" Kenton oozed with pride. I couldn't believe what I saw! He stood beside a glistening green pine. He had seen beneath the dead needles, beyond its dispensability, to behold its potential.

We still have the tree. It stands in the yard all year as a silent reminder to have hope. At Christmastime we bring in our tree, decorate it with bright and beautiful ornaments, and celebrate the birth of Christ, the birth of hope.

I am the resurrection and the life.

JOHN 11:25

SEEK AND YE SHALL FIND

Dianna Hutts Aston

THE SKY WAS a dingy sheet of gloom, and it was wet and cold the January afternoon I sat in Barbara's office, staring out the window. Raindrops dripped from leafless branches. Rivulets of water ran like tears down the windowpanes. I sighed, drooping under the weight of winter's longest weeks.

"I wish it was still Christmas," I murmured.

"You do?" Barbara said, and I thought she sounded surprised.

"Yes," I said, as if I were stating the obvious. Didn't everybody long for the bright lights of Christmas at this dismal time of year?

Barbara was a psychotherapist, a wise woman whose counsel I had sought more than a year earlier for a tangle of problems I couldn't sort out on my own.

"What is it about Christmas you love?" she asked.

My mind filled with images of dark nights and pretty lights, Santa flying across the sky, a pile of presents under the tree, cookies and fudge, feasts and family, songs about the little Lord Jesus laying down his sweet head.

I tried to put my visions and the feeling they inspired into words, but even that took more effort than I could summon. Thankfully, she knew what I was trying to say.

Eyebrows drawn, she looked at me thoughtfully, gathering her words. "Dianna," she said, and a long pause filled the air, "it's our job to find the Christmas in every day."

I felt as if she'd lassoed me with a string of lights and brought me up short. It was a twinkling moment of revelation. I realized that I longed for the love and joy that is so visible at Christmastime, the love and joy that wraps around you like a warm coat on a snowy day. What I had yet to discover was that every day is a gift, with moments of love and joy for us to unwrap and look upon with expectation and delight.

Barbara's words settled into my heart and became my carol, and I saw the world with new eyes.

Now, I look for Christmas in every day and most days I find it—on the soft cheeks of my children and in their backyard laughter, in the six wrinkles that appear on my husband's forehead when he sees that I've strung Christmas lights around the window in July, and in my old dog's smile when I drive up.

Still, there are days when I can't see past the gray slush of January, and on those days, I pull out another string of lights and wind it around the silk ficus tree in my room, pour myself a cup of coffee in my red Christmas mug, and remember Barbara's words: "It's our job to find the Christmas in every day."

Be joyful always.
1 Thessalonians 5:16

THIRSTY

Joann Olson

I HAVE TRIED every trick in the book: Cut the trunk. Add sugar to the water. Don't add anything to the water. Buy the tree early. Buy the tree late. No matter what I do, my Christmas tree stops "drinking" water. The first week of January finds me dragging an extremely dry Christmas tree out of the house, strewing needles everywhere.

One year, I noticed that my Christmas tree didn't look that bad—as long as I kept my distance. The lights all worked, the ornaments were beautiful, and the garland was placed perfectly. From across the room, the tree seemed to be doing fine. But up close I could see that it was brittle and dropping needles.

I sat for a while and pondered that tree. How could it look so good from across the room and so pathetic up close? Why did it stop drinking water? And then came another thought: I felt just like that tree. Like my Christmas tree, I looked "just fine" from a distance. All the lights and garland in my life—daily work and ministry activities—were placed

173

just right. But spiritually, I had stopped "drinking" and my soul had dried up, just as the Christmas tree had. The dried-out Christmas tree had to be thrown out. Would God throw me out, or could he somehow restore my soul?

Psalm 65 describes "streams of God" filled with water that drench the land and soften it, bringing God's abundance and bounty. I realized that I needed to start drinking again from the streams of God: reading the Bible, praying, and allowing him to bring renewal. I decided that I also needed something that regularly reminds me to check my "water level."

Each January, the ritual of putting on a heavy sweatshirt and gloves serves as my reminder. As I haul the tree to the curb, I examine my heart for areas that are drying up, and I ask God to begin the necessary restoration. And throughout the year—whenever my toe finds a stray dried-up pine needle, hidden deep in the living room carpet—I am reminded to check it once again.

You care for the land and water it; you enrich it abundantly. The streams of God are filled with water to provide the people with grain, for so you have ordained it. You drench its furrows and level its ridges; you soften it with showers and bless its crops. You crown the year with your bounty, and your carts overflow with abundance.

PSALM 65:9–11

CHRISTMAS STOLEN

Karen Igla

WHY DO I ALWAYS GET *in the checkout lane that has a problem?* This time the checker was a trainee. His trainer, a pretty girl whose face was pinched with the strain of her patience, was meticulously checking each price entry he made.

Trying to restrain my own impatience, I dug in my purse for my shopping list. I had spent too much time in this hobby store. Thinking of the other stores I wanted to visit, I noticed it was already dark outside.

"That comes to $34.17," she said.

Although I had bought the least expensive of the choices, the total was still more than I should have spent. *I'm supposed to watch my budget better than this,* I thought as I tucked the receipt into my purse.

I picked up my two small plastic bags of Christmas tree decorations and walked to my husband's worn but faithful '87 Sentra.

Setting the bags on the passenger seat, I drove to the grocery store. I got out, leaving the car unlocked as I normally do. Then I hesitated. A thought grazed my mind. *What if someone should steal those bags?*

That is ridiculous, I rebutted. *Who would expect anything worth stealing in this old car? Besides, it's so dark no one would see the bags anyway.*

When I returned to the car with my groceries, the bags were gone.

"I can't believe it!" I slapped my palms on the steering wheel.

With disgust, I thought about what kind of person would steal Christmas decorations. Well, there was no use in broiling in my anger. I knew God would deal with whomever had been so brazen.

Immediately, I felt chagrin for having ignored the Holy Spirit's prompting to protect those bags.

"I'm sorry I was careless with your things, Lord," I repented.

Wearily, I finished my other shopping before returning to the hobby store to purchase more of the same items. Fatigue clouded my efforts to remember what exactly I had bought and in what aisles I had found the items. With only half the items in my cart, I spied the girl who had been training the checker.

"Do you remember me?" I asked. "I was here earlier buying these things. Now I'm back because someone stole them from my car."

"No, I don't remember you," she said. Then, peering into my cart, she exclaimed, "It's the same stuff!" Turning, she headed to the back of the store. "Wait here," she called over her shoulder. "My manager needs to talk to you!"

Soon she returned with a tall, young man. "Are you buying these things?" he asked.

"Yes, I am," I replied and told him what had happened.

"A woman was in here just a little while ago trying to return these items. She insisted that she had just been through the line."

"Is she still here?"

"No, she left saying she would be back tomorrow." He looked back down at the items in my cart and gave a short, cynical laugh. "They always get nervous when you ask them about the receipt." Then, he looked at me and smiled. "Well, I have your stuff."

Did I hear right?

"I have your stuff," he repeated.

"I have the receipt." I dug into my purse and produced the proof of purchase.

The manager examined the receipt. "Wait here. I'll be back with your bags."

"Oh, thank you, Lord!" I exclaimed. "God took care of me. God watched out for me!"

At my outburst, the people in the nearby checkout line craned their necks in my direction. Smiling, the checker returned to her register. They could not know that the geyser of joy springing from my heart was only partly due to having my things restored. It was also the overwhelming sense that God keeps charge over all that concerns me.

I winged home. Briskly, the lights and ornaments were hung. And, last of all, the plastic crystal star was placed atop the tree. At that moment, my three children arrived home from their outing with Daddy.

They squealed with delight when they saw the newly adorned tree.

"Listen! Let me tell you what God did for us tonight!"

After I related the story, we gave thanks and admired the tree. The decorations were among the cheapest the store offered, but to me they will always be priceless.

> *The LORD is good, a refuge in times*
> *of trouble. He cares for those who*
> *trust in him.*
>
> NAHUM 1:7

THE CHRISTMAS ROBE

Valerie D. Howe

ONE CHRISTMAS, my father and I decided to select a needy family from a local charity and give them food and gifts. We were excited, not only to purchase these special Christmas items, but also to deliver them. The agency gave us a card with information about the family's needs and wants. The woman of the family wanted a new robe in a medium size. While shopping at the outlet mall, I saw a green woman's robe, trimmed in gold braid. It was not expensive, but very pretty, so I bought it, thinking what a lovely gift it would be.

A few days before Christmas, my father and I arrived with a generous supply of food and gifts for the family. I was so proud of myself, thinking how like Jesus I was being, especially with the Christmas robe. I thought of the verse Matthew 25:40, ". . . whatever you did for one of the least of these brothers of mine, you did for me." But my thoughts were only making *me* feel good. I don't believe they impressed God at all. What I thought was the "Christmas spirit" was merely smugness that I must be a pretty fine person, unlike the least of these people I was helping. I was soon to find out that I was the least.

When we began to unload the articles from the car, a large woman stepped into the doorway. I was disappointed, because I knew the medium-sized robe would surely not fit her. I slipped the gift back into the car, so she would not see it. Although we had brought many other gifts for her and the family, I was aggravated that I had bought the robe. What would I do with it now?

We continued to bring in the rest of the gifts, spoke a few minutes with the family, who was at least grateful, and I thought my charitable Christmas deed was done.

But on Christmas Eve, just as we were supposed to be going to my parents' family celebration, my husband, Kenny, announced that we were going to see Mildred at the nursing home. Mildred was a family friend who had no children or husband or family. Within thirty minutes we were to be at my parents' across town, and I became very irritated.

"Kenny," I griped, "we are going to be late if we do that and I don't want everybody to have to wait on us. Besides, I don't want to take the kids out there." We had four children under the age of eight, anxious to celebrate Christmas.

Kenny firmly stated, "Valerie, we need to go see her and I can't believe that we can't give her a few minutes. We have five places to go to exchange gifts, and Mildred doesn't have anywhere to go for Christmas. And can you find her a present to wrap up?"

My attitude was to "just forget it," and the kids joined in with my sentiment. "No, Daddy," they whined. "We want to go to Grandma and Grandpa's!"

Very begrudgingly, I looked for an appropriate item and the only thing I could find unmarked under the tree was the still gift-wrapped green robe. I wasn't sure it would fit her, but after we loaded all the presents for our family gift exchange, I put the green robe in the car, hoping Kenny would change his mind. He didn't.

I didn't say a great deal on the way to the nursing home (the silent treatment, you know). I think I might have muttered something about being late once or twice and said we really had to hurry. The kids were still on my side.

We arrived and found Mildred's room. She hadn't heard us enter, so Kenny gently roused her by tapping her back. By now I was acting hospitable and kind, but inside I was still in a hurry. My heart was beginning to soften, though, because I was looking at a frail little woman who had no one to celebrate Christmas with tonight.

I handed her the gift box. She opened it with a sparkle in her eyes as if to say, "For me?" She pulled out the green robe and immediately put it on over her clothes. With tears streaming down her cheeks she said, "I wouldn't have gotten a Christmas present at all if you hadn't come."

The gold braiding reflected like glitter around her face. While Mildred may have appeared to me earlier as "the least of these," I now saw her as a great woman.

Oh, how small I felt! Now I knew exactly who was least. It was me. For you see, at that moment it no longer mattered whether we were late for Christmas dinner, or the family celebration, or the gift exchange, because now I was awakened to what true giving was all about. My arrogance and pride fell as I gazed at her in that Christmas robe. Oh, how I wished I had been a cheerful giver.

As we began to leave, Mildred gave our children oranges and candy—all she *thought* she had to give. However, she also unknowingly gave me the gift which I desperately needed that night: the gift of humility. This was the very gift that Jesus gave so many years ago when he left behind his kingly robe and was born in a manger.

I asked God to forgive my pride and then I looked at Mildred one final time as we said good-bye and "Merry Christmas." I can't tell you how grateful I was that we had come. God had intended for Mildred to have that robe all along.

> *And being found in appearance*
> *as a man, he humbled himself and*
> *became obedient to death—even*
> *death on a cross!*
>
> PHILIPPIANS 2:8

Sweet Sounds
of Gratitude

Sandra J. Bunch

A NUMBER OF YEARS AGO, my husband and I were
"volunteered" by the members of our Sunday school
class to deliver food the class had collected for a family during the holiday season. This family lived in a
rough part of town, and I wasn't happy about going
there. I also questioned whether they were actually
needy and wondered if they could be looking for a
handout—or worse yet, a vulnerable victim. A head-
line flashed before my eyes: "Good Samaritan Slain
in Exchange for Christmas Dinner."

In the interest of self-preservation, I had a plan
in the back of my fearful mind. My husband, Rick,
would have to take in the packages alone while I
waited in the car. They wouldn't dare attack a man
of his stature.

Upon arriving at the house, I surveyed the sur-
roundings. The small, fenced-in yard did not ap-

pear to have anyone lurking in its shadows, and the tiny house was well lighted. My fear had diminished somewhat, so I decided that I would help carry in the food. Surely with the two of us working together, we'd be on our way in no time. I just wanted to go home.

We were greeted at the door by a friendly middle-aged couple. Behind them, six children gathered to welcome us into their home. We greeted them in return and I smiled the best I could, hoping it would cover my nervousness.

Rick and I set the first load on the table. I remained cautious as I glanced around the room. The furniture was mismatched and worn. The walls were in need of fresh paint, and I saw no modern conveniences. I felt ashamed as the extent of their need became very apparent.

The two teenaged sons helped the father carry in the remaining packages. The two elementary-aged boys began to rummage through them. My heart broke as I witnessed their excitement.

"Look, Mom! Milk!"

"Sugar!" exclaimed another as he jumped up and down hugging the bag to his chest. Stunned, I stood there silently as reality hit me. I hurried toward the door, anxious to get into the car where my tears could flow freely. My feet would not carry me fast enough as I wished them all a happy holiday.

The father's voice stopped me, "Please, sit down. We have something for you." *What in the world could they possibly give us?* I thought to myself. I reluctantly sat down next to Rick and waited as the six children left the room. Rick, knowing how anxious I was,

WITH
THE DAWN
OF REDEEMING
GRACE

184

squeezed my hand and gave me a reassuring look. I hoped it would not take long.

Soon the four boys, now accompanied by their two teenaged sisters, filed back in. They formed a semi-circle around us. Then the most beautiful gift, in the form of two songs, was presented to us. Their voices, blending in perfect harmony, were bathed in sweet sounds of gratitude. My heart was warmed and my spirit touched by the beauty of their serenade. The tears of guilt that had clouded my vision now sprang forth. I sat there ashamed that I had doubted the motives of this family. I immediately thanked God for the privilege of such an experience.

Shortly, we were back in our car heading home. I closed my eyes and smiled as I replayed the music in my head. Their faces, full of thankfulness and appreciation, became permanently etched in my mind. We came to give to them, but they gave us much, much more. They blessed us with their gratitude. I turned to Rick and said, "I want God to use me to bless people in that way."

That desire has led me beyond the perimeters of my comfort zone many times. Now, we coordinate our church's holiday basket program, which provides food for more than twenty families each year. Although I would prefer to stay within the walls of predictability, I know that God uses us best when we are willing to step out and follow where he leads—especially when we don't know what we'll find when we get there.

I will give you a new heart and put a new spirit in you; I will remove from you your heart of stone and give you a heart of flesh.

EZEKIEL 36:26

THE MUTT
AND THE
GOLDEN RETRIEVER

Cynthia Schaible Boyll

I HAVE ALWAYS BELIEVED good observation keeps daily
life from becoming mundane. I notice when the Gil-
fillans get a new front door or the Chastains replace
their mailbox. I do not consider this neighborly nosi-
ness, since it is all in public view. Plus, occasionally
something really worthwhile occurs, like what I observed a few Christmases ago.

It was a gloomy Advent for me—too many loved
ones had died or were sick or going through difficulties. I just could not get myself revved up for "Ho!
Ho! Ho!" and frosted sugar cookies. Yet mild depression did not totally dull my observation skills. I was
intrigued by the growing Christmas-light competition
in our neighborhood.

Then there was the golden retriever puppy, tethered in the Connors' front yard. According to my children's school bus sources, he had cost a lot and was an early Christmas present. Shortly after his Advent arrival, a homely, dirty mutt started hanging around the beautiful golden retriever. Whenever I drove by, the two could be seen outside, one tethered and one not. Not long after both of their arrivals, dozens of little flags appeared bordering the Connors' yard. We surmised the golden retriever was getting invisible fencing. Would that discourage the stray dog?

The next day my children came home from the bus and announced that the Connors had indeed gotten rid of a dog. *Poor homely mutt,* I thought, hoping that, even though he was ugly, somebody at the animal shelter might adopt him for Christmas.

The next day, however, a surprise awaited me when I drove out of our neighborhood. There, standing proudly in the Connors' yard, was not the golden retriever, but the lowly mutt, bathed and groomed, with a big red collar around his neck.

It seemed the golden retriever was returned to the breeders for a more acceptable home, but "Smoky" somehow wagged his way into the family's hearts. The sudden adoption made what had been a discouraging season for me a more hopeful one. I was reminded that I had every reason to hope for a bright future, for I am not an orphan, but a child of God. Smoky is still in the Connors' yard, and I recently noticed he has been joined by another mutt, who also wears a big red collar. Truly, there is a place for us all.

But when the time had fully come,
God sent his Son, born of a woman,
born under law, to redeem those
under law, that we might receive the
full rights of sons. Because you are
sons, God sent the Spirit of his Son
into our hearts, the Spirit who calls
out, "Abba, Father." So you are no
longer a slave, but a son; and since you
are a son, God has made you also an
heir.

GALATIANS 4:4–7

SAVED

Cheryl Kirking

"I MAY HAVE A STORY for your book, Cheryl." I had just finished making a presentation at a women's event and had told the audience that I was compiling this book of Christmas stories. She had been lingering near the table where I was signing books, and I could see she wanted to wait until the crowd had dwindled.

She was in her midsixties, trim and attractive, with perfectly coiffed, silver hair, and wearing a stylish navy pantsuit. I smiled enthusiastically. "Well, great! Tell me!" I urged.

"No. There are so many women who still want to speak with you—I don't want to monopolize your time." She leaned close, almost whispering. "When you're done here, could you meet with me in the lounge by the library? It won't take long."

"Okay!" I whispered back with a smile.

After greeting the few remaining women, I left my husband, who had traveled with me, to pack up our sound equipment. I wandered down the deserted hallways to the library lounge where she was waiting, as promised.

"Hi!" I said and smiled, extending my hand. "I'm sorry. I didn't catch your name . . ."

"It's Joanna," she replied, squeezing my hand. "I appreciate your staying late. I know you must be tired. But I didn't want to take you away from the others. And . . ." she glanced at the door, "I really don't want anyone to overhear."

She smoothed her slacks and examined her manicured nails. Looking up, she smiled. "After I tell you my story, you'll understand why I don't want anyone to overhear."

I nodded, trying my best to look understanding. "Well," she began with a sigh. "I've never told anyone this, but I have wanted to. It's not something I'm proud of, but, in a strange way, I'm glad it happened."

I nodded again, my curiosity piqued.

"It happened almost thirty years ago, in mid-December. It was three days before my husband's company Christmas party. I was doing a little shopping and feeling sorry for myself, I guess. I couldn't buy the cocktail dress I had wanted and would wear an 'old' dress to the party instead. My husband owned his own company then, and business had not been good that year. He felt like a failure, and I was frustrated that he had given all the employees a raise the year before, and yet we were struggling to maintain our current lifestyle. And our lifestyle was a struggle to maintain even in a good year." She smiled wryly. "We tended to live *far* beyond our means.

"Well," she continued, "as I was Christmas shopping, I thought I'd take a peek at the jewelry counter, and I spotted a gold cloisonné bangle bracelet. Not solid gold, probably gold-plated, but with a lovely enameled design. It wasn't terribly expensive, maybe thirty dollars.

"I certainly didn't need it. But I *felt* like I *needed* it—needed something new, just for *me*. I don't know how else to explain it. I just felt that I *deserved* that bracelet!

"And, Cheryl," she said as she looked at me intensely. "I *took* the bracelet! Just slipped it on and went about my shopping. I almost . . . *almost* . . . left the store with it on. The voice inside me kept saying 'Joanna, this isn't like you! It isn't right!' But I kept it on, until my conscience got the better of me and I decided to put it back. As I was hanging it back on the display rack, I jumped at the sound of a man's voice. 'So, you decided against the bracelet?' A man in a brown jacket was suddenly standing right next to me. My nerves were completely rattled, but I tried to appear nonchalant as I asked, 'I beg your pardon?' And he answered, 'I noticed you are putting that bracelet back.'

"I tried to sound innocent, but I was stammering, 'Yes, well . . . I had tried it on, you see . . . and I forgot I was wearing it.' He gave me this look, this incriminating look, and said, 'Uh-huh . . . well, I'm glad you remembered to put it back.'

"I was *furious* at his insinuation! Oh, I was indignant! As I turned to storm away, he repeated, '*Really*, ma'am, I'm *really* glad you decided to put it back.' This time his voice was soft . . . forgiving. It was like he was looking directly into my soul.

"He must have worked for the store's security. He must have seen me take it! I was that close to being arrested for shoplifting!" She held her thumb and forefinger a quarter-inch apart. "And for what? A little bracelet!

"I don't even remember driving home, but when I got there, I just fell through the kitchen doorway and collapsed onto the floor. Just crumbled, my forehead on the floor, and kept saying, 'Oh God, oh God, oh God.' Thinking over and over how I could have been arrested, how my reputation would have been ruined, how stupid I was, how *angry* I was at that security guy . . . and at myself. I was just shaking, shivering, repeating in disbelief, 'Oh God, oh God, oh God!'

"Then after five, maybe ten, minutes my words took on a different tone. 'Oh *God!*' My words became a cry to the Almighty. 'Oh God! Oh God! Oh *God!*' I was crying out for forgiveness, asking him to help erase my haughtiness, begging him to come and fill the void that I foolishly thought a new dress and jewelry might fill. But I think I knew, deep down, it wasn't about the bracelet. It was about so, so much *more* that was missing in my life! I promised him I'd change. I asked *him* to change *me.* I was so ashamed, and yet . . . an incredible feeling of relief flooded over me. I knew that I was *forgiven*. Forgiven, not just for the bracelet incident, but for *all* my sins. My cry became words of humility and gratitude. Words of praise! 'Oh *God,* Oh *God,* Oh *God!*'

"So . . ." She sighed, dropping her hands on her lap. "That's my Christmas story. Not just because it happened at Christmastime, but because it's when

Jesus came to me, like he came to the world at Christmas."

"Or maybe the day you came to *him*," I pondered quietly.

"Yes! Yes—that's exactly how it was!" she exclaimed. "I came to him and made a promise, and accepted his promise. He saved me from . . . myself. Saved me from an empty life. I am so much more . . ." She searched for the word. "So much more . . . *compassionate* now. I realize that my weaknesses are no less sinful than those of others who have more 'obvious' faults. I'm not proud of my story, but I think it has a purpose. I don't know what you might want to do with it, but if you think it might help somebody, you can use it however you wish. Maybe you can find a way to make it seem . . . interesting."

"Oh, I think it's plenty interesting, Joanna," I said, giving her a hug. "And thank you for sharing your story. I know it will touch people's hearts."

It had already touched mine. It reminded me that we have a great God, who loved the world so much that he gave his only Son. A Savior who came to us as a humble baby. Accessible, that we might come to him to receive his promise of forgiveness, of love, and of eternity. Who hears us when we humbly cry out, *"Oh God!"*

If my people, who are called by my name, will humble themselves and pray and seek my face and turn from their wicked ways, then will I hear from heaven and will forgive their sin and will heal their land. Now my eyes will be open and my ears attentive to the prayers offered.

2 Chronicles 7:14–15

What can I give him, poor as I am?
If I were a shepherd, I would bring a lamb;
If I were a wise man, I would do my part;
Yet what can I give him? Give him my heart.

CHRISTINA G. ROSSETTI
(FROM THE CAROL "IN THE BLEAK MIDWINTER")

Contributors

All of the stories included in this book have been used by permission of the authors. All rights reserved. For permission to use any of these stories, please contact the original source.

Charlotte Adelsperger, with her daughter Karen Hayse, co-authored a gift book for mothers, *Through the Generations: The Unique Call of Motherhood* (Beacon Hill Press). She is a popular speaker and has written for more than seventy magazines, including *Woman's World*. Her poem, *Christmas Came* ©1985 Charlotte Adelsperger, was first published in *Decision* magazine. Contact: 11629 Riley, Overland Park, KS 66210-2254

Dianna Hutts Aston has worked as a journalist and editor and has a degree in journalism from the University of Houston. She writes from her home in Central Texas, where she lives with her husband, David; her children, James and Elizabeth; and an old dog, Bear.

Beverly M. Bartlett, a native San Franciscan, lived in Germany for five years with her husband. Learning German and making lasting friendships in many countries was an enriching experience. Now in Cleveland, Ohio, with her husband, Tim, and Pekingese dog, Muffin, she's a professional organizer. Her story has been previously published.

Irene Bastian is a teacher/farmer/writer who resides on a family grain farm with her husband and two children near the Foothills of Alberta, Canada. She believes God uses our life experiences to teach us lessons that help us better serve others. Contact: bastianp@fclc.com

Cynthia Schaible Boyll writes in Loveland, Ohio, where she lives with husband, Chuck, and their children, Ben and Leah. She would like readers to know she prays for her neighbors as well as observing their front yards!

Sandra J. Bunch and her husband, Rick, are parents of Aimee and Elisabeth. They are involved in family ministry and teach at marriage seminars. Sandra has been published by DaySpring greeting cards and in the book *Treasures of a Woman's Heart* (Starburst). Contact: APensPal@aol.com

Pat A. Carman is a freelance writer and editor of a community newspaper that she and her husband, Ken, own in Salem, Oregon. With a wide range of interests she writes stories, articles, and women's devotionals. A real estate broker, she works with "women in transition." Contact: primroselane@compuserve.com

John W. Doll began writing lyrics in Chicago for Lawrence Welk. He continued writing after moving to California. A prolific writer, he is a regular contributor to the *Chicken Soup for the Soul* series. He lives on an orange grove with his wife, Lanie. To order John's book, *Autumn Leaves Around the World*, contact him at 2377 Grand Ave., Fillmore, CA 93015.

Bill Egan, a retired U.S. Navy photojournalist, is a correspondent for *The Daytona Beach News-Journal* and provides Christmas research for Charles Osgood of "The Osgood File" on the *CBS Radio Network, CBS Radio News,* and *The New York Times.* He is one of the world's leading experts on the origin of the carol "Silent Night." In December 2000 he was presented with Austria's highest civilian award, the Gold Medal of Honor of the Republic of Austria.

Marjorie K. Evans, a former elementary school teacher, is now a freelance writer with many published articles. She and her husband Edgar enjoy grandparenting, church, reading, their Welsh

corgi, gardening, and raising orchids. Contact: 4162 Fireside Circle, Irvine, CA 92604-2216

Raymond Flagg Jr., now retired, taught industrial arts for thirty-nine years. During that time he developed and taught a home-steading course in a rural Maine public high school for nineteen years, teaching students to make use of local resources in practical ways. This true story, *Full Circle,* still brings tears to his eyes when relating it.

Cheryl Herndon is a certified nurse-midwife living in Florida. Married for thirty years, she has two married children and two grandchildren. She is the founder of WomanKind, a service organization providing spiritual, physical, and emotional support to women of all ages.

Valerie D. Howe is currently a household executive with five children, one husband, and one dog, in addition to her writing and speaking career. Contact: P.O. Box 141, Lebanon, MO 65536. E-mail: vhowe@llion.org, or fax: (417) 532-4282

Liz Hoyt is a freelance writer in the Texas Hill Country. Besides raising a teenage grandson, she is a busy volunteer and illuminates life through her stories of the heart. Contact: 106 Seamoor, Fredericksburg, TX 78624, or mehoyt@fbg.net

Karen Igla enjoys being a pastor's wife, home-educating their three children, and freelance writing. When not wielding a pen, she brandishes a shovel in the garden or powers up the drill for a remodeling project at their home in Overland Park, Kansas. Contact: igla@netzero.net

Linda LaMar Jewell is a published writer and CLASS graduate. Teaching letter-writing and journaling workshops, her motto is: "Someone you know longs to receive a letter—it's a letter only you can write." To book Linda for a workshop, contact CLASServices at (505) 899-4283 or spkrsrvcs@aol.com.

Cheryl Kirking compiled this book and is the author of *Ripples of Joy* (Shaw/Waterbrook Press). A conference speaker and song-writer, she presents her Ripplemaker™ Keynotes in Concert nationwide. For more information, see page 205. For booking, or to order CDs or tapes, visit www.cherylkirking.com.

Carmen Leal is a speaker, singer, and author of *Faces of Huntington's; Pinches of Salt, Prisms of Light;* and *WriterSpeaker.Com,* a marketing and research Internet guide for writers and speakers. Contact: Carmen@writerspeaker.com or www.writerspeaker.com

Jan Leong discovered writing while undertaking the classical education of her children at home. Lauren, Kenton, Constance, Mason, and husband, Terry, offer encouragement as she teaches and facilitates writing seminars equipping the body of Christ to write effectively for God's service and glory. Contact: tjleong@juno.com

Patricia Lorenz is an inspirational/humor writer and speaker. She's the author of *Stuff That Matters for Single Parents* and *A Hug a Day for Single Parents* and a contributor to nine *Chicken Soup for the Soul* books. More than four hundred of her nonfiction articles have appeared in seventy publications, including *Reader's Digest, Guideposts, Working Mother,* and *Single-Parent Family.* Contact: 7457 S. Pennsylvania Ave., Oak Creek, WI 53154. E-mail: patricialorenz@juno.com

Karin McClain writes family stories to give her younger siblings, children, and grandchildren a feeling of connection and identification with previous generations. Contact: 330 Gamble St., Shelby, OH 44875

James A. McClung is a United Methodist pastor in Richmond, Virginia. He is the founder of Camp Rainbow Connections, a camp for mentally disabled adults. A writer and songwriter, he is currently working on a book of his experiences.

Mary Linn McClure has a bachelor of arts degree from Park University with a major in library science. She works in a library and lives in Kansas City, Missouri. Contact: MaryJDI@aol.com

Louisa Godissart McQuillen's latest project is When Seasons Change, a chapbook of autumn-Christmas-winter poetry and stories. Replete with artwork and photography, it is endorsed

by the Pennsylvania Poetry Society: "This one will help you get through winter." Send $5 plus $1 s/h to 525 Decatur St., Philipsburg, PA 16866-2609 or contact Louisa at LZM4@psu.edu.

Roberta L. Messner is a registered nurse, quality management specialist, speaker, and author of more than a thousand stories and articles and several books. She is a regular contributor to *Guideposts*, and her work has appeared in *Chicken Soup for the Soul* books. Her medical, inspirational, and home decorating articles have appeared in more than one hundred publications.

Lynn D. Morrissey is editor of the best-selling *Seasons of a Woman's Heart* (Starburst) and the sequel, *Treasures of a Woman's Heart*. She has contributed to numerous best-selling devotional books and is a CLASSpeaker and staff member. She specializes in prayer-journaling and women's topics. Contact: http://members.primary.net/~lynnswords/

Brenda Nixon works with churches to attract and minister to parents. She is a wife, mother of two, professional speaker, and author of *Parenting Power in the Early Years* (WinePress). For speaking engagements, Brenda may be contacted through her web site: www.parentpwr.com or by calling (816) 361-9811.

Joann Olson works on staff with The Navigators at the University of Wisconsin-Eau Claire, where she mentors college students in their spiritual walk. Before joining The Navigators in 1999, Joann worked as a computer trainer, network administrator, and technical writer in Michigan.

Patricia A. Perry's work has appeared in *The War Cry, Rolling Stone* magazine, *Keys for Kids*, and elsewhere. She was the winner of the 1997 NOVA Christian Writers Fellowship Marjorie Holmes Writing Contest. She edits "Ink and the Spirit," the newsletter of Capital Christian Writers.

Kathleen Boratko Ruckman is a freelance writer, women's Bible study teacher, and mother of four. Her short stories and articles have appeared in numerous magazines and short story anthologies. She and her husband, Tom, and family reside in Eugene, Oregon, in the beautiful Willamette Valley.

Jessie Schut has taught professionally, and is now a writer. She has written many articles for a variety of publications, as well as two books of devotions. Her latest book *How to Have a Great Sunday School* will be available from CRC Publications in the fall of 2001. She lives in Edmonton, Alberta,Canada.

David Michael Smith is a lifelong resident of Georgetown, Delaware, and enjoys writing Christian fiction. His story *Unlikely Angel* is dedicated to the memory of Bill Whelen Sr. His first novel, *The Invitation*, a supernatural thriller, was published by iUniverse.com. He plans to release a book of self-penned Christmas stories. Contact: davidandgeri@hotmail.com

JudyAnn Squier has been a public speaker since the age of thirteen, with writing a more recent avocation. She resides in northern California with her husband, David, and their three daughters.

B. J. Taylor teaches a class for writers, heads a critique group in southern California, and has published a book that helps writers develop their own writers' group. She contributes regularly to a local magazine and has been published in newspapers and books. Contact: bjtaylor3@earthlink.net

Susan M. Warren is a mother of four children, career missionary with SEND International in Khabarovsk, Russia, and published author of numerous devotionals, articles, and short stories. Contact: susanwarren@mail.com

Jeannie S. Williams is a writer, speaker, and magician, and has entertained audiences for years with her special blend of creativity and humor. She is author of the children's book *What Time Is Recess?* (Craftmasters Books) and a frequent contributor to the *Chicken Soup for the Soul* series and other books. She is founder of Unlock the Magic creative writing workshops. Contact: P.O. Box 1476, Sikeston, MO 63801

Margolyn Woods is a former Rose Bowl Queen and actress who now lives in Oklahoma with her husband and three children. She is the author of seven books and a popular speaker for women's retreats and conferences all over the country.

Cheryl Kirking tickles the funny bones and tugs at the heartstrings of audiences nationwide by weaving home-spun humor, common sense, and original songs into her Ripples Unlimited™ Keynotes, concerts, and workshops. Known as a *Ripplemaker™*, Cheryl encourages others to identify, develop, and use their talents for the good of others.

Cheryl has given hundreds of presentations for associations, hospitals, women's conferences, school districts, parenting groups, and churches. She draws upon her professional background in high-school teaching, public relations, and lay ministry. She is an alumnus of the University of Wisconsin-Madison and a member of the National Speakers Association.

She is the author of the book *Ripples of Joy,* and has recorded six CDs of original songs on the Mill Pond Music label—but she considers her triplets her greatest production!

Her greatest joy is being Mom to Blake, Sarah Jean, and Bryce. They keep her days slightly chaotic and her heart delightfully full. She shares life with them and her husband, David Kilker, in a house by the woods.

To contact Cheryl Kirking, please write to:

Ripples Unlimited™
P.O. Box 525
Lake Mills, WI 53551
or visit her web site at www.cherylkirking.com